HONEST TO GOD

PUBLISHER'S NOTE

THE success and impact of Bishop John A. T. Robinson's *Honest to God* far exceeded what anyone expected when it was published in North America and Great Britain in 1963. The book catapulted into public debate and became "one of the most widely discussed religious writings of the century and more than a million copies were sold" (John Macquarrie, *Twentieth Century Religious Thought*, rev. ed. [New York: Charles Scribner's Sons, 1981], 396).

This book helped popularize the views of three twentieth-century theologians: Dietrich Bonhoeffer, Rudolf Bultmann, and Paul Tillich. Robinson translated their views on God, the Bible, Jesus Christ, and the life of the Christian into a wide-ranging critique of long-established doctrinal formulations in the church. He did not believe that merely restating traditional orthodoxy in modern terms was adequate. "A much more radical recasting," he judged, "is demanded, in the process of which the most fundamental categories of our theology—of God, of the supernatural, and of religion itself—must go into the melting" (preface). To convey central doctrines of Christian faith in contemporary and "nonmythological" ways was a primary goal. The result was a blockbuster book that drew a mass readership on both sides of the Atlantic.

This 40th Anniversary Edition is supplemented by the reflections of two respected theologians. Douglas John Hall considers the significance of *Honest to God* in North America while Rowan Williams discusses the reception of *Honest to God* in Great Britain. These essays help put this work in perspective and explore the importance of this volume for a new generation of readers.

Honest to God

40th Anniversary Edition

JOHN A. T. ROBINSON

With Essays by
Douglas John Hall and Rowan Williams

Westminster John Knox Press
LOUISVILLE • LONDON

© 1963 SCM Press

© 2002 The Estate of John A. T. Robinson

"*Honest to God* in Great Britain" © 2002 Westminster John Knox Press

"*Honest to God* in North America" © 2002 Westminster John Knox Press

Honest to God was first published in Great Britain in 1963 by SCM Press.

Honest to God was first published in North America in 1963 by The Westminster Press.

Scripture quotations from the Revised Standard Version of the Bible are copyright © 1946, 1952, 1971, and 1973 by the Division of Christian Education of the National Council of the Churches of Christ in the U.S.A. and are used by permission.

Scripture quotations from *The New English Bible* are copyright © by The Delegates of the Oxford University Press and The Syndics of the Cambridge University Press, 1961, 1970. Used by permission.

Cover design by Eric Handel/LMNOP
Cover art by McKenzie: *The Competitor,* 1906 (bronze). Courtesy of The Bridgeman Art Library

40th anniversary edition
Published by Westminster John Knox Press
Louisville, Kentucky

This book is printed on acid-free paper that meets the American National Standards Institute Z39.48 standard. ∞

PRINTED IN THE UNITED STATES OF AMERICA

02 03 04 05 06 07 08 09 10 11 — 10 9 8 7 6 5 4 3 2 1

Library of Congress Cataloging-in-Publication Data is on file at the Library of Congress, Washington, D.C.

ISBN 0-664-22422-9

CONTENTS

FOR

STEPHEN AND CATHERINE

AND THEIR GENERATION

PREFACE

IT belongs to the office of a bishop in the Church to be a guardian and defender of its doctrine. I find myself a bishop at a moment when the discharge of this burden can seldom have demanded greater depth of divinity and quality of discernment.

For I suspect that we stand on the brink of a period in which it is going to become increasingly difficult to know what the true defence of Christian truth requires. There are always those (and doubtless rightly they will be in the majority) who see the best, and indeed the only, defence of doctrine to lie in the firm reiteration, in fresh and intelligent contemporary language, of 'the faith once delivered to the saints'. And the Church has not lacked in recent years theologians and apologists who have given themselves to this task. Their work has been rewarded by a hungry following, and there will always be need of more of them. Nothing that I go on to say should be taken to deny their indispensable vocation.

At the same time, I believe we are being called, over the years ahead, to far more than a restating of traditional orthodoxy in modern terms. Indeed, if our defence of the Faith is limited to this, we shall find in all likelihood that we have lost out to all but a tiny religious remnant. A much more radical recasting, I would judge, is demanded, in the process of which the most fundamental categories of our theology—of God, of the supernatural, and of religion itself—must go into the melting. Indeed, though we shall not of course be able to do it, I can at least understand what those mean who urge that we should do well to give up using the word 'God' for a generation, so impregnated has it become with a way of thinking we may have to discard if the Gospel is to signify anything.

For I am convinced that there is a growing gulf between the traditional orthodox supernaturalism in which our Faith has been framed and the categories which the 'lay' world (for want of a better term) finds meaningful today. And by that I do not mean there is an increasing gap between Christianity and pagan society. That may well be so, but this is not the divide of which I am speaking. For it is not a division on the truth of the Gospel itself. Indeed, many who are Christians find themselves on the same side as those who are not. And among one's intelligent non-Christian friends one discovers many who are far nearer to the Kingdom of heaven than they themselves can credit. For while they imagine they have rejected the Gospel, they have in fact largely been put off by a particular way of thinking about the world which quite legitimately they find incredible.

Moreover, the line to which I am referring runs right through the middle of myself, although as time goes on I find there is less and less of me left, as it were, to the right of it. Thus, not infrequently, as I watch or listen to a broadcast discussion between a Christian and a humanist, I catch myself realizing that most of my sympathies are on the humanist's side. This is not in the least because my faith or commitment is in doubt, but because I share instinctively with him his inability to accept the scheme of thought and mould of religion within which alone that Faith is being offered to him. I feel he is *right* to rebel against it, and I am increasingly uncomfortable that 'orthodoxy' should be identified with it.

What this structure is must be left for further designation

to the body of the book. My only concern here is to plead for the recognition that those who believe their share in the total apologetic task of the Church to be a radical questioning of the established 'religious frame' should be accepted no less as genuine and, in the long run equally necessary, defenders of the Faith.

But I am not sanguine. I am inclined to think that the gulf must grow wider before it is bridged and that there will be an increasing alienation, both within the ranks of the Church and outside it, between those whose basic recipe is the mixture as before (however revitalized) and those who feel compelled above all to be honest *wherever* it may lead them. I believe, regretfully, that Dr Alec Vidler's conclusion in a recent broadcast,[1] which was bitterly attacked, is only too true: 'We've got a very big leeway to make up, because there's been so much suppression of real, deep thought and intellectual alertness and integrity in the Church.' I am not in the least accusing of dishonesty those who find the traditional framework of metaphysics and morals entirely acceptable (I do so with a large part of myself). What dismays me is the vehemence—and at bottom the insecurity—of those who feel that the Faith can only be defended by branding as enemies within the camp those who do not.

I believe there are all too uncomfortable analogies to the ecclesiastical scene of a hundred years ago, when (as we now recognize) the guardians of traditional orthodoxy all but rendered impossible the true defence of the Gospel. When we consider the distance we have all moved since then,[2] we can see that almost everything said from within

[1] BBC/TV Sunday, November 4, 1962.
[2] Cf., e.g., P. O. G. White, 'The Colenso Controversy', *Theology*, lxv (October 1962), pp. 402-8.

the Church at the time has since proved too conservative. What I have tried to say, in a tentative and exploratory way, may seem to be radical, and doubtless to many heretical. The one thing of which I am fairly sure is that, in retrospect, it will be seen to have erred in not being nearly radical enough.

November 1962　　　　　　　　　JOHN WOOLWICH

1

RELUCTANT REVOLUTION

Up There or Out There?

THE Bible speaks of a God 'up there'. No doubt its picture of a three-decker universe, of 'the heaven above, the earth beneath and the waters under the earth', was once taken quite literally. No doubt also its more sophisticated writers, if pressed, would have been the first to regard this as symbolic language to represent and convey spiritual realities. Yet clearly they were not pressed. Or at any rate they were not oppressed by it. Even such an educated man of the world as St Luke can express the conviction of Christ's ascension —the conviction that he is not merely alive but reigns in the might and right of God—in the crudest terms of being 'lifted up' into heaven, there to sit down at the right hand of the Most High.[1] He feels no need to offer any apology for this language, even though he of all New Testament writers was commending Christianity to what Schleiermacher called its 'cultured despisers'. This is the more remarkable because, in contrast, he leaves his readers in no doubt that what we might regard as the scarcely more primitive notions of God entertained by the Athenians,[2] that the deity lives in temples made by man and needs to be served by human hands, were utterly superseded by Christianity.

Moreover, it is the two most mature theologians of the New Testament, St John and the later Paul, who write most uninhibitedly of this 'going up' and 'coming down'.

[1] Acts 1.9-11. [2] Acts 17.22-31.

No one has ascended into heaven but he who descended from heaven, the Son of man.[1]

Do you take offence at this? Then what if you were to see the Son of man ascending where he was before?[2]

In saying, 'He ascended', what does it mean but that he had also descended into the lower parts of the earth? He who descended is he who also ascended far above all the heavens, that he might fill all things.[3]

They are able to use this language without any sense of constraint because it had not become an embarrassment to them. Everybody accepted what it meant to speak of a God up there, even though the groundlings might understand it more grossly than the gnostics. For St Paul, no doubt, to be 'caught up to the third heaven'[4] was as much a metaphor as it is to us (though for him a considerably more precise metaphor). But he could use it to the spiritually sophisticated at Corinth with no consciousness that he must 'demythologize' if he were to make it acceptable.

For the New Testament writers the idea of a God 'up there' created no embarrassment—because it had not yet become a difficulty. For us too it creates little embarrassment—because, for the most part, it has ceased to be a difficulty. We are scarcely even conscious that the majority of the words for what we value most are still in terms of height, though as Edwyn Bevan observed in his Gifford Lectures,[5] 'The proposition: Moral and spiritual worth is greater or less in ratio to the distance outwards from the earth's surface, would certainly seem to be, if stated nakedly like that, an odd proposition.' Yet it is one that we have long ago found it unnecessary to explain away. We may indeed continue to have to tell our children that heaven is

[1] John 3.13.   [2] John 6.61 f.   [3] Eph. 4.9 f.   [4] II Cor. 12.2.
[5] *Symbolism and Belief* (1938), p. 30. Chs. II and III on 'Height' are a *locus classicus* for the conception of God 'up there'.

not in fact over their heads nor God literally 'above the bright blue sky'. Moreover, whatever we may accept with the top of our minds, most of us still retain deep down the mental image of 'an old man in the sky'. Nevertheless, for most of us most of the time the traditional language of a three-storeyed universe is not a serious obstacle. It does not worry us intellectually, it is not an 'offence' to faith, because we have long since made a remarkable transposition, of which we are hardly aware. In fact, we do not realize how crudely spatial much of the Biblical terminology is, for we have ceased to perceive it that way. It is as though when reading a musical score what we actually saw was not the notes printed but the notes of the key into which mentally we were transposing it. There are some notes, as it were, in the Biblical score which still strike us in the old way (the Ascension story, for instance) and which we have to make a conscious effort to transpose, but in general we assimilate the language without trouble.

For in place of a God who is literally or physically 'up there' we have accepted, as part of our mental furniture, a God who is spiritually or metaphysically 'out there'. There are, of course, those for whom he is almost literally 'out there'. They may have accepted the Copernican revolution in science, but until recently at any rate they have still been able to think of God as in some way 'beyond' outer space. In fact the number of people who instinctively seem to feel that it is no longer possible to believe in God in the space-age shows how crudely physical much of this thinking about a God 'out there' has been. Until the last recesses of the cosmos had been explored or were capable of being explored (by radio-telescope if not by rocketry), it was still possible to locate God mentally in some *terra incognita*. But now it seems there is no room for him, not merely in the inn, but in the entire universe: for there are no vacant places left. In reality, of course, our new view of the universe has made not the slightest difference. Indeed, the limit set to 'space' by the speed of light (so that beyond a certain point—not all that much further than our present range—everything recedes over the horizon of visibility) is even more severe. And there is nothing to stop us, if we wish to, locating God 'beyond' it. And there he would be quite invulnerable—in a 'gap' science could never fill. But in fact the coming of the space-age has destroyed this crude projection of God—and for that we should be grateful. For if God is 'beyond', he is not *literally* beyond anything.

But the idea of a God spiritually or metaphysically 'out there' dies very much harder. Indeed, most people would be seriously disturbed by the thought that it should need to die at all. For it *is* their God, and they have nothing to put in its place. And for the words 'they' and 'their' it would be more honest to substitute 'we' and 'our'. For it is the God of our own upbringing and conversation, the God of our fathers and of our religion, who is under attack. Every one of us lives with some mental picture of a God 'out there', a God who 'exists' above and beyond the world he made, a God 'to' whom we pray and to whom we 'go' when we die. In traditional Christian theology, the doctrine of the Trinity witnesses to the self-subsistence of this divine Being outside us and apart from us. The doctrine of creation asserts that at a moment of time this God called 'the world' into existence over against himself. The Biblical record describes how he proceeds to enter into contact with those whom he has made, how he establishes a 'covenant' with them, how he 'sends' to them his prophets, and how in the fullness of time he 'visits' them in the person of his Son, who must one day 'come again' to gather the faithful to himself.

This picture of a God 'out there' coming to earth like some visitor from outer space underlies every popular presentation of the Christian drama of salvation, whether from the pulpit or the presses. Indeed, it is noticeable that those who have been most successful in communicating it in our day—Dorothy Sayers, C. S. Lewis, J. B. Phillips—have hesitated least in being boldly anthropomorphic in the use of this language. They have not, of course, taken it literally, any more than the New Testament writers take literally the God 'up there', but they have not apparently felt it any embarrassment to the setting forth of the Gospel. This is sufficient testimony to the fact that there is a ready-made public for whom this whole frame of reference still presents no difficulties, and their very achievement should make us hesitate to pull it down or call it in question.

Indeed, the last thing I want to do is to appear to criticize from a superior position. I should like to think that it were possible to use this mythological language of the God 'out there' and make the same utterly natural and unself-conscious transposition as I have suggested we already do with the language of the God 'up there'. Indeed, unless we become used to doing this and are able to take this theological notation, as it were, in our stride, we shall cut ourselves off from the classics of the Christian faith, just as we should be unable to read the Bible were we to stumble at *its* way of describing God. I believe, however, that we may have to pass through a century or more of reappraisal before this becomes possible and before this language ceases to be an offence to faith for a great many people. No one wants to live in such a period, and one could heartily wish it were not necessary. But the signs are that we are reaching the point at which the whole conception of a God 'out there', which has served us so well since the collapse of the three-decker universe, is itself becoming more of a hindrance than a help.

In a previous age there came a moment when the three-decker likewise proved an embarrassment, even as a piece of mental furniture. But in this case there was a considerable interval between the time when it ceased to be taken literally as a model of the universe and the time when it ceased to perform a useful function as a metaphor. An illustration of this is to be seen in the doctrine of hell. In the old scheme, hell was 'down there'. By Shakespeare's time no one thought of it as literally under the earth, but still in *Hamlet* it is lively and credible enough as a metaphor. But a localized hell gradually lost more and more of its purchase over the imagination, and revivalist attempts to stoke its flames did not succeed in restoring its power. The tragedy in this instance is that no effective translation into terms of the God 'out there' was found for the Devil and his angels, the pit and the lake of fire. This element therefore tended to drop out of popular Christianity altogether—much to the detriment of the depth of the Gospel.

But the point I wish to make here is that the supersession of the old scheme was a gradual one. After it had been discredited scientifically, it continued to serve theologically as an acceptable frame of reference. The image of a God 'up there' survived its validity as a literal description of reality by many centuries. But today I believe we may be confronted by a double crisis. The final psychological, if not logical, blow delivered by modern science and technology to the idea that there might *literally* be a God 'out there' has *coincided* with an awareness that the *mental* picture of such a God may be more of a stumbling-block than an aid to belief in the Gospel. There is a double pressure to discard this entire construction, and with it any belief in God at all.

Moreover, it is not merely a question of the speed of adjustment required. The abandonment of a God 'out there' represents a much more radical break than the transition to this concept from that of a God 'up there'. For this earlier transposition was largely a matter of verbal notation, of a change in spatial metaphor, important as this undoubtedly was in liberating Christianity from a flat-earth cosmology. But to be asked to give up any idea of a Being 'out there' at all will appear to be an outright denial of God. For, to the ordinary way of thinking, to believe in God means to be convinced of the existence of such a supreme and separate Being. 'Theists' are those who believe that such a Being exists, 'atheists' those who deny that he does.

But suppose such a super-Being 'out there' is really only a sophisticated version of the Old Man in the sky? Suppose belief in God does not, indeed cannot, mean being persuaded of the 'existence' of some entity, even a supreme entity, which might or might not be there, like life on Mars? Suppose the atheists are right—but that this is no more the end or denial of Christianity than the discrediting of the God 'up there', which must in its time have seemed the contradiction of all that the Bible said? Suppose that all such atheism does is to destroy an idol, and that we can and must get on without a God 'out there' at all? Have we seriously faced the possibility that to abandon such an idol may in the future be the only way of making Christianity meaningful, except to the few remaining equivalents of flat-earthers (just as to have clung earlier to the God 'up there' would have made it impossible in the modern world for any but primitive peoples to believe the Gospel)? Perhaps after all the Freudians are right, that such a God— the God of traditional popular theology—*is* a projection, and perhaps we are being called to live without that projection in any form.

That is not an attractive proposition: inevitably it feels like being orphaned. And it is bound to be misunderstood and resisted as a denial of the Gospel, as a betrayal of what the Bible says (though actually the Bible speaks in literal terms of a God whom we have already abandoned). And it will encounter the opposition not only of the fundamentalists but of 90 per cent of Church people. Equally it will be resented by most unthinking non-churchgoers, who tend to be more jealous of the beliefs they have rejected and deeply shocked that they should be betrayed. Above all, there is the large percentage of oneself that finds this revolution unacceptable and wishes it were unnecessary.

This raises again the insistent question, Why? Is it really necessary to pass through this Copernican revolution? Must we upset what most people happily believe—or happily choose not to believe? And have we anything to put in its place?

Some Christian Questioners

In some moods, indeed, I wonder. But I know in my own mind that these are questions that must be explored. Or rather, they are questions that are already being explored on many sides. The only issue is whether they remain on the fringe of the intellectual debate or are dragged into the middle and placed squarely under men's noses. I know that as a bishop I could happily get on with most of my work without ever being forced to discuss such questions. I could keep the ecclesiastical machine going quite smoothly, in fact much more smoothly, without raising them. The kind of sermons I normally have to preach do not require one to get within remote range of them. Indeed, such is the pressure of regular priorities that I should not have been able, let alone obliged, to let them occupy my mind for long enough to write this, were it not that I was forcibly laid up for three months. But they were questions that had long been dogging me, and I felt from the beginning the spiritual necessity laid upon me to use this period to allow them their head.

The only way I can put it is to say that over the years a number of things have unaccountably 'rung a bell'; various unco-ordinated aspects of one's reading and experience have come to 'add up'. The inarticulate conviction forms within one that certain things are true or important. One may not grasp them fully or understand why they matter. One may not even welcome them. One simply knows that if one is to retain one's integrity one must come to terms with them. For if their priority is sensed and they are not attended to, then subtly other convictions begin to lose their power: one continues to trot these convictions out, one says one believes in them (and one does), but somehow they seem emptier. One is aware that insights that carry their own authentication, however subjective, are not being allowed to modify them.

And then, equally, there are certain other things which have *not* rung a bell, certain areas of traditional Christian expression—devotional and practical—which have evidently meant a great deal for most people but which have simply left one cold. The obvious conclusion is that this is due to one's own spiritual inadequacy. And there is clearly a very large amount of truth in this. But I have not forgotten the relief with which twenty years ago, back at my theological college, I discovered in a conversation of the small hours a kindred spirit, to whom also the whole of the teaching we received on prayer (as it happened to be in this case) meant equally little. There was nothing about it one could say was wrong. Indeed, it was an impressive roundabout: but one was simply not on it—and, what was worse, had no particular urge to be. To realize that after all one might not be the chief of sinners, or the only man out of step, lifted a load of secret, yet basically unadmitted, guilt. And since then I have found others—and in each situation a surprisingly large minority—who confess to the same blind spot. The traditional material is all true, no doubt, and one recognizes it as something one ought to be able to respond to, but somehow it seems to be going on around one rather than within. Yet to question it openly is to appear to let down the side, to be branded as hopelessly unspiritual, and to cause others to stumble.

And this is only one particular instance. Indeed, as one goes on, it is the things one doesn't believe and finds one doesn't have to believe which are as liberating as the things one does. James Pike, the Bishop of California, is one who has admitted to finding the same. In a stimulating—and thoroughly constructive—article,[1] which rocked the American Church and even drew the charge of heresy from the clergy of one diocese, he wrote: 'I stand in a religious tradition . . . which really does not know very much about religion. The Roman Catholics and the Southern Baptists know a great deal more about religion than we do. And . . . I feel that many people within my own church—and some of them write tracts for the book-stalls of churches—know too many answers. I do not deny the truth of these answers; I simply don't know as much as the authors of the pamphlets.'

But the point I want to make is that I gradually came to

[1] 'Three-pronged Synthesis', *The Christian Century*, December 21, 1960.

realize that some of the things that rang bells and some of the things that didn't seemed to be connected. I began to find that I was questioning one whole set of presuppositions and feeling towards another in its place. All I am doing in this book is to try to think this process aloud and help to articulate it for others. For I believe it is a process common in some form or other to many in our age. Indeed, it is the number of straws apparently blowing in the same direction that strikes me as significant. I have done little more than pick a few of them up and I am conscious that in this book, more than in any other I have written, I am struggling to think other people's thoughts after them. I cannot claim to have understood all I am trying to transmit. And it is for this reason partly that I have chosen to let them speak, through extended quotations, in their own words. But it is also because I see this as an attempt at communication, at mediation between a realm of discourse in which anything I have to say is very familiar and unoriginal and another, popular world, both within and without the Church, in which it is totally unfamiliar and almost heretical.

At this stage, to indicate what I am talking about, let me instance three pieces of writing, all brief, which contain ideas that immediately found lodgement when I first read them and which have since proved seminal not only for me but for many of this generation.

The first of these in date for me (though not in composition) was a sermon by Paul Tillich, which appeared in his collection *The Shaking of the Foundations*, published in England in 1949.[1] It was called 'The Depth of Existence' and it opened my eyes to the transformation that seemed to come over so much of the traditional religious symbolism

[1] Now available in a Pelican edition (1962), to which the page references are given.

when it was transposed from the heights to the depths. God, Tillich was saying, is not a projection 'out there', an Other beyond the skies, of whose existence we have to convince ourselves, but the Ground of our very being.

> The name of this infinite and inexhaustible depth and ground of all being is *God*. That depth is what the word *God* means. And if that word has not much meaning for you, translate it, and speak of the depths of your life, of the source of your being, of your ultimate concern, of what you take seriously without any reservation. Perhaps, in order to do so, you must forget everything traditional that you have learned about God, perhaps even that word itself. For if you know that God means depth, you know much about him. You cannot then call yourself an atheist or unbeliever. For you cannot think or say: Life has no depth! Life is shallow. Being itself is surface only. If you could say this in complete seriousness, you would be an atheist; but otherwise you are not. He who knows about depth knows about God.[1]

I remember at the time how these words lit up for me. I did what I have never done before or since: I simply read Tillich's sermon, in place of an address of my own, to the students I was then teaching. I do not remember looking at the words again till I came to write this, but they formed one of the streams below the surface that were to collect into the underground river of which I have since become conscious. I shall return to them, as to the other influences I mention in this chapter, subsequently. Here it is enough to say they seemed to speak of God with a new and indestructible relevance and made the traditional language of a God that came in from outside both remote and artificial.

Next, I must register the impact of the now famous passages about 'Christianity without religion' in Dietrich

[1] *Op. cit.*, pp. 63 f.

Bonhoeffer's *Letters and Papers from Prison*.[1] I first encountered extracts from these in *The Ecumenical Review* for
January 1952, shortly after their first publication in German.
One felt at once that the Church was not yet ready for what
Bonhoeffer was giving us as his last will and testament
before he was hanged by the S.S.: indeed, it might be
understood properly only a hundred years hence. But it
seemed one of those trickles that must one day split rocks.
Hitherto, Bonhoeffer was saying, the Church has based its
preaching of the Gospel on the appeal to religious experience, to the fact that deep down every man feels the need
for religion in some form, the need for a God to whom to
give himself, a God in terms of whom to explain the world.
But suppose men come to feel that they can get along perfectly well without 'religion', without any desire for personal
salvation, without any sense of sin, without any need of
'that hypothesis'? Is Christianity to be confined to those who
still have this sense of insufficiency, this 'God-shaped blank',
or who can be induced to have it? Bonhoeffer's answer was
to say that God is deliberately calling us in this twentieth
century to a form of Christianity that does not depend on
the premise of religion, just as St Paul was calling men in
the first century to a form of Christianity that did not
depend on the premise of circumcision.

What that meant I hardly began to understand. But I
knew that this was something we must learn to assimilate:
the system could not simply eject it. And now after a bare
decade it feels as if we have been living with it for very much
longer.

Then, thirdly, there was an essay which created an almost
immediate explosion when it appeared in 1941, though I

[1] Ed. E. Bethge (1953; 2nd ed.—to which all references are made—
1956). The American edition is entitled *Prisoner for God*.

did not read it in detail till it was translated into English in 1953. This was the manifesto by Rudolf Bultmann entitled, 'New Testament and Mythology'.[1]

Once more Bultmann seemed to be putting a finger on something very near the quick of the Gospel message. For when he spoke of the 'mythological' element in the New Testament he was really referring to all the language which seeks to characterize the Gospel history as *more* than bare history like any other history. The importance of this 'plus' is that it is precisely what makes events of two thousand years ago a preaching or gospel for today at all. And his contention was that this whole element is unintelligible jargon to the modern man. In order to express the 'trans-historical' character of the historical event of Jesus of Nazareth, the New Testament writers used the 'mythological' language of pre-existence, incarnation, ascent and descent, miraculous intervention, cosmic catastrophe, and so on, which according to Bultmann, make sense only on a now completely antiquated world-view. Thus, modern man, instead of stumbling on the real rock of offence (the scandal of the Cross), is put off by the very things which *should* be translating that historical occurrence into an act of God for him, but which in fact merely make it incredible. The relevance of Bultmann's analysis and of his programme of 'demythologizing' to the whole question of God 'out there' from which we started is obvious enough. If he is right, the entire conception of a supernatural order which invades and 'perforates'[2] this one must be abandoned. But if so, what do we mean by God, by revelation, and what becomes of Christianity?

---

[1] *Kerygma and Myth* (ed. H. W. Bartsch), Vol. i, pp. 1-44.
[2] The phrase is used by Bultmann in a subsequent and more popular presentation of his thesis, *Jesus Christ and Mythology* (1960), p. 15.

Theology and the World

Now all these three writers might appear to have been raising theological issues fairly far removed from the everyday concerns of ordinary men. But what convinced me of their importance was not simply the spark they struck in myself. It was that for all their apparent difficulty and Teutonic origin they so evidently spoke not only to intelligent non-theologians but to those in closest touch with the unchurched masses of our modern urban and industrial civilization. Tillich is one of the few theologians to have broken through what he himself calls, in another connection, 'the theological circle'. Bonhoeffer is talked of where 'religion' does not penetrate, and the kind of ideas he threw out have been taken up by two men, the Bishop of Middleton[1] and Dr George Macleod,[2] who are as exercised as any in our generation by the relation of theology to the real world. Again, I was astonished to discover how Bultmann's ideas, for all their forbidding jargon, seemed to come like a breath of fresh air to entirely untheological students. Indeed, he had in the first instance been driven to them by the practical impossibility of communicating the Gospel to soldiers at the front. And one of my valued possessions is a copy of a letter written by Bultmann to the Sheffield Industrial Mission, setting out with a profound simplicity the Gospel as he would present it to steel-workers in a demythologized form.

Moreover, though I said earlier that such thinking would be rejected and resented by those who had turned their backs on Christianity, I find that it comes with refreshing

[1] E. R. Wickham, *Church and People in an Industrial City* (1957), pp. 232-8.
[2] *Only One Way Left* (1956; 2nd ed. 1958).

relevance to many who have nothing to undo. It seems to speak far more directly to their entirely non-religious experience than the traditional 'popular' apologetic.

Nevertheless, despite its practical reference, such thinking is still nowhere near being assimilated or digested by the ordinary man in the pew, nor by most of those who preach to him or write for him. I believe there must come a time when in some form or another it will be so digested, and when our everyday thinking about God will have become as subtly transformed by it as by the earlier transposition of which I have spoken. But that is probably not the task of this generation. The first stage is to get it out of the world of the professional theologians into that of the intelligent thinking churchman—so that, for instance, one could presuppose that it was deeply affecting the way doctrine was taught in our theological colleges and lay training courses: indeed, I suspect that its relevance may be more immediately sensed for the development of a genuinely lay theology.

One test is how long it takes really to become Anglicized. For it has not as yet seriously influenced the main stream of English theology or churchmanship.[1] To take an extreme but not unrepresentative example, I doubt whether any sign of it could be traced in however prolonged a perusal of *The Chronicle of the Convocation of Canterbury*. And this is not simply a factious allusion. For I am not writing this book as a professional theologian: indeed, this is not my own academic field. I am deliberately writing as an ordinary

[1] For a pioneering attempt to bring home its relevance, see R. Gregor Smith, *The New Man: Christianity and Man's Coming of Age* (1956). In the few months since this was first written there have been signs of a rapidly quickening interest. Cf. D. Jenkins, *Beyond Religion* (1962), and A. R. Vidler, 'Religion and the National Church', in *Soundings* (ed. A. R. Vidler, 1962). F. G. Downing, 'Man's Coming of Age', *Prism*, December 1962, pp. 33-42, is most penetrating.

churchman, and one moreover who is very much an 'insider' as far as church membership is concerned.

I stress this standpoint because I find myself coming to so many of the same conclusions, though from a completely opposite direction, as a fellow Anglican, Dr John Wren-Lewis, a young industrial scientist and lay theologian, whose pungent criticisms of the contemporary religious scene in articles and broadcasts have attracted some attention in recent years. He has recorded his spiritual pilgrimage in his contribution to the collection of essays edited by Dewi Morgan, *They Became Anglicans*. Apart from the fact that we were both born in Kent within a few years of each other, our paths could hardly have been more different. I was born into the heart of the ecclesiastical 'establishment'—the Precincts at Canterbury: he was the son of a plumber, brought up as an outsider to the Church and its whole middle-class ethos. He is a scientist, a layman, a convert. I am not a scientist; I never seriously thought of being anything but a parson; and, however much I find myself instinctively a radical in matters theological, I belong by nature to the 'once-born' rather than to the 'twice-born' type. I have never really doubted the fundamental truth of the Christian faith—though I have constantly found myself questioning its expression.

Yet for this very reason I may be in the better position to convince the ordinary middle-of-the-road man, who accepts without too much difficulty the things that I accept, that we really are being called to a 'Copernican revolution'. None of us enjoys that, and I am only too conscious of the forces of inertia within myself. It is for me a reluctant revolution, whose full extent I have hardly begun to comprehend. I am well aware that much of what I shall seek to say will be seriously misunderstood, and will doubtless deserve to be.

Yet I feel impelled to the point where I can no other. I do not pretend to know the answers in advance. It is much more a matter of sensing certain things on the pulses, of groping forward, almost of being pushed from behind. All I can do is to try to be honest—honest to God and about God—and to follow the argument wherever it leads.

THE END OF THEISM?

Must Christianity be 'Supranaturalist'?

TRADITIONAL Christian theology has been based upon the proofs for the existence of God. The presupposition of these proofs, psychologically if not logically, is that God might or might not exist. They argue from something which everyone admits exists (the world) to a Being beyond it who could or could not be there. The purpose of the argument is to show that he must be there, that his being is 'necessary'; but the presupposition behind it is that there is an entity or being 'out there' whose existence is problematic and has to be demonstrated. Now such an entity, even if it could be proved beyond dispute, would not be God: it would merely be a further piece of existence, that might conceivably not have been there—or a demonstration would not have been required.

Rather, we must start the other way round. God is, by definition, ultimate reality. And one cannot argue whether ultimate reality *exists*. One can only ask what ultimate reality is like—whether, for instance, in the last analysis what lies at the heart of things and governs their working is to be described in personal or impersonal categories. Thus, the fundamental theological question consists not in establishing the 'existence' of God as a separate entity but in pressing through in ultimate concern to what Tillich calls 'the ground of our being'.

What he has to say at this point is most readily summarized in the opening pages of the second volume of his *Systematic*

Theology,[1] where he restates the position he has argued in the first volume and defends it against his critics.

The traditional formulation of Christianity, he says, has been in terms of what he calls 'supranaturalism'. According to this way of thinking, which is what we have all been brought up to, God is posited as 'the highest Being'—out there, above and beyond this world, existing in his own right alongside and over against his creation. As Tillich puts it elsewhere, he is

> a being beside others and as such part of the whole of reality. He certainly is considered its most important part, but as a part and therefore as subjected to the structure of the whole . . . He is seen as a self which has a world, as an ego which is related to a thou, as a cause which is separated from its effect, as having a definite space and an endless time. He is a being, not being-itself.[2]

The caricature of this way of thinking is the Deist conception of God's relation to the world. Here God is the supreme Being, the grand Architect, who exists somewhere out beyond the world—like a rich aunt in Australia—who started it all going, periodically intervenes in its running, and generally gives evidence of his benevolent interest in it.

It is a simple matter to shoot down this caricature and to say that what *we* believe in is not Deism but Theism, and that God's relationship to the world is fully and intimately personal, not this remote watchmaker relationship described by the Deists. But it is easy to modify the *quality* of the relationship and to leave the basic structure of it unchanged, so that we continue to picture God as a Person, who looks down at this world which he has made and loves from 'out there'. We know, of course, that he does not exist in space.

[1] Vol. ii (1957), pp. 5-11. The date, as in the case of other American books, refers, where available, to the first British edition.
[2] *The Courage to Be* (1952), p. 175.

But we think of him nevertheless as defined and marked off from other beings *as if* he did. And this is what is decisive. He is thought of as *a* Being whose separate existence over and above the sum of things has to be demonstrated and established.

It is difficult to criticize this way of thinking without appearing to threaten the entire fabric of Christianity—so interwoven is it in the warp and woof of our thinking. And, of course, it *is* criticized by those who reject this supra-naturalist position as a rejection of Christianity. Those who, in the famous words of Laplace to Napoleon, 'find no need of this hypothesis' attack it in the name of what they call the 'naturalist' position. The most influential exponent of this position in England today, Professor Julian Huxley, expressly contrasts 'dualistic supernaturalism' with 'unitary naturalism'.[1] The existence of God as a separate entity can, he says, be dismissed as superfluous; for the world may be explained just as adequately without positing such a Being.

The 'naturalist' view of the world identifies God, not indeed with the totality of things, the universe, *per se*, but with what gives meaning and direction to nature. In Tillich's words,

> The phrase *deus sive natura*, used by people like Scotus Erigena and Spinoza, does not say that God is identical with nature but that he is identical with the *natura naturans*, the creative nature, the creative ground of all natural objects. In modern naturalism the religious quality of these affirmations has almost disappeared, especially among philosophising scientists who understand nature in terms of materialism and mechanism.[2]

Huxley himself has indeed argued movingly for religion[3] as a necessity of the human spirit. But any notion that God

[1] *The Observer*, Sunday July 17, 1960, p. 17.
[2] *Systematic Theology*, vol. ii, p. 7.
[3] *Religion without Revelation* (1927; 2nd ed. 1957).

really exists 'out there' must be dismissed: 'gods are peripheral phenomena produced by evolution'.[1] True religion (if that is not a contradiction in terms, as it would be for the Marxist) consists in harmonizing oneself with the evolutionary process as it develops ever higher forms of self-consciousness.

'Naturalism' as a philosophy of life is clearly and consciously an attack on Christianity. For it 'the term "God" becomes interchangeable with the term "universe" and therefore is semantically superfluous'.[2] But the God it is bowing out is the God of the 'supranaturalist' way of thinking. The real question is how far Christianity is identical with, or ultimately committed to, this way of thinking.

Must Christianity be 'Mythological'?

Undoubtedly it has been identified with it, and somewhere deep down in ourselves it still is. The whole world-view of the Bible, to be sure, is unashamedly supranaturalistic. It thinks in terms of a three-storey universe with God up there, 'above' nature. But even when we have refined away what we should regard as the crudities and literalism of this construction, we are still left with what is essentially a mythological picture of God and his relation to the world. Behind such phrases as 'God created the heavens and the earth', or 'God came down from heaven', or 'God sent his only-begotten Son', lies a view of the world which portrays God as a person living in heaven, a God who is distinguished from the gods of the heathen by the fact that 'there is no god beside me'.

In the last century a painful but decisive step forward was taken in the recognition that the Bible does contain 'myth',

[1] *The Observer*, *ibid.*   [2] Tillich, *ibid.*

and that this is an important form of religious truth. It was gradually acknowledged, by all except extreme fundamentalists, that the Genesis stories of the Creation and Fall were representations of the deepest truths about man and the universe in the form of myth rather than history, and were none the less valid for that. Indeed, it was essential to the defence of Christian truth to recognize and assert that these stories were *not* history, and not therefore in competition with the alternative accounts of anthropology or cosmology. Those who did not make this distinction were, we can now see, playing straight into the hands of Thomas Huxley and his friends.

In this century the ground of the debate has shifted—though in particular areas of Christian doctrine (especially in that of the last things[1]) the dispute that raged a hundred years ago in relation to the first things has still to be fought through to its conclusion, and the proper distinction established between what statements are intended as history and what as myth. But the centre of today's debate is concerned not with the relation of particular myths to history, but with how far Christianity is committed to a mythological, or supranaturalist, picture of the universe at all. Is it necessary for the Biblical faith to be expressed in terms of this world-view, which in its way is as primitive philosophically as the Genesis stories are primitive scientifically? May it not be that the truth of Christianity can be detached from the one as much as from the other—and may it not be equally important to do so if it is to be defended properly today? In other words, is the reaction to naturalism the rehabilitation of supranaturalism, or can one say that Julian Huxley is performing as valuable a service in detaching Christianity from the latter as we now see his

[1] See my book *In the End, God . . .* (1950).

grandfather was in shaking the Church out of its obscurantism in matters scientific?

This is the problem to which Bultmann has addressed himself. And he answers boldly, 'There is nothing specifically Christian in the mythical view of the world as such. It is simply the cosmology of a pre-scientific age.'[1] The New Testament, he says, presents redemption in Christ as a supranatural event—as the incarnation from 'the other side' of a celestial Being who enters this earthly scene through a miraculous birth, performs signs and wonders as an indication of his heavenly origin, and after an equally miraculous resurrection returns by ascent to the celestial sphere whence he came. In truth, Bultmann maintains, all this language is not, properly speaking, describing a supranatural transaction of any kind but is an attempt to express the real depth, dimension and significance of the *historical* event of Jesus Christ. In this person and event there was something of ultimate, unconditional significance for human life—and that, translated into the mythological view of the world, comes out as 'God' (a Being up there) 'sending' (to 'this' world) his only-begotten 'Son'. The transcendental significance of the historical event is 'objectivized' as a supranatural transaction.

I do not wish here to be drawn into the controversy which Bultmann's programme of demythologizing has provoked.[2] Much of it has, I believe, been due to elements in his presen-

---

[1] *Kerygma and Myth*, vol. i, p. 3.
[2] The main debate can be followed in *Kerygma and Myth*, ed. H. W. Bartsch (vol. i, 1953; vol. ii, 1962). The more important books in English include: I. Henderson, *Myth in the New Testament* (1952); H. W. Owen, *Revelation and Existence* (1957); L. Malevez, *The Christian Message and Myth* (1958); G. Miegge, *Gospel and Myth* (1960); J. Macquarrie, *The Scope of Demythologizing* (1960); D. Cairns, *A Gospel without Myth?* (1960); S. M. Ogden, *Christ without Myth* (1962).

tation which are to some extent personal and fortuitous. Thus,

(a) Bultmann is inclined to make statements about what 'no modern man' could accept (such as 'It is impossible to use electric light and the wireless and believe . . .') which reflect the scientific dogmatism of a previous generation. This gives to some of his exposition an air of old-fashioned modernism.

(b) The fact that he regards *so much* of the Gospel history as expendable (e.g. the empty tomb *in toto*) is due to the fact that purely in his capacity as a New Testament critic he is extremely, and I believe unwarrantably, distrustful of the tradition. His historical scepticism is not necessarily implied in his critique of mythology.

(c) His heavy reliance on the particular philosophy of (Heidegger's) Existentialism as a replacement for the mythological world-view is historically, and indeed geographically, conditioned. He finds it valuable as a substitute for the contemporary generation in Germany; but we are not bound to embrace it as the only alternative.

One of the earliest and most penetrating criticisms of Bultmann's original essay was made by Bonhoeffer, and to quote it will serve as a transition to his own contribution. 'My view of it today', he writes from prison in 1944,

would be not that he went too far, as most people seem to think, but that he did not go far enough. It is not only the mythological conceptions such as the miracles, the ascension and the like (which are not in principle separable from the conceptions of God, faith and so on) that are problematic, but the 'religious' conceptions themselves. You cannot, as Bultmann imagines, separate God and miracles, but you do have to be able to interpret and proclaim *both* of them in a 'non-religious' sense.[1]

[1] *Op. cit.*, p. 125.

Must Christianity be 'Religious'?

What does Bonhoeffer mean by this startling paradox of a non-religious understanding of God?[1]

I will try to define my position from the historical angle. The movement beginning about the thirteenth century (I am not going to get involved in any arguments about the exact date) towards the autonomy of man (under which head I place the discovery of the laws by which the world lives and manages in science, social and political affairs, art, ethics and religion) has in our time reached a certain completion. Man has learned to cope with all questions of importance without recourse to God as a working hypothesis. In questions concerning science, art, and even ethics, this has become an understood thing which one scarcely dares to tilt at any more. But for the last hundred years or so it has been increasingly true of religious questions also: it is becoming evident that everything gets along without 'God', and just as well as before. As in the scientific field, so in human affairs generally, what we call 'God' is being more and more edged out of life, losing more and more ground.

Catholic and Protestant historians are agreed that it is in this development that the great defection from God, from Christ, is to be discerned, and the more they bring in and make use of God and Christ in opposition to this trend, the more the trend itself considers itself to be anti-Christian. The world which has attained to a realization of itself and of the laws which govern its existence is so sure of itself that we become frightened. False starts and failures do not make the world deviate from the path and development it is following; they are accepted with fortitude and detachment as part of the bargain, and even an event like the present war is no

[1] I have made no attempt to give a balanced picture of Bonhoeffer's theology as a whole, which cannot be done by concentrating, as I have been compelled to do, on this final flowering of it. See J. D. Godsey, *The Theology of Dietrich Bonhoeffer* (1960); E. Bethge, 'The Challenge of Dietrich Bonhoeffer's Life and Theology', *Chicago Theological Seminary Register*, vol. li (February, 1961), pp. 1-38 (for the best brief introduction); *The Place of Bonhoeffer* (ed. Martin E. Marty; 1963).

exception. Christian apologetic has taken the most varying forms of opposition to this self-assurance. Efforts are made to prove to a world thus come of age that it cannot live without the tutelage of 'God'. Even though there has been surrender on all secular problems, there still remain the so-called ultimate questions—death, guilt—on which only 'God' can furnish an answer, and which are the reason why God and the Church and the pastor are needed. Thus we live, to some extent by these ultimate questions of humanity. But what if one day they no longer exist as such, if they too can be answered without 'God'? . . .

The attack by Christian apologetic upon the adulthood of the world I consider to be in the first place pointless, in the second ignoble, and in the third un-Christian. Pointless, because it looks to me like an attempt to put a grown-up man back into adolescence, i.e. to make him dependent on things on which he is not in fact dependent any more, thrusting him back into the midst of problems which are in fact not problems for him any more. Ignoble, because this amounts to an effort to exploit the weakness of man for purposes alien to him and not freely subscribed to by him. Un-Christian, because for Christ himself is being substituted one particular stage in the religiousness of man.[1]

Bonhoeffer speaks of the God of 'religion' as a *deus ex machina*. He must be 'there' to provide the answers and explanations beyond the point at which our understanding or our capacities fail. But such a God is constantly pushed further and further back as the tide of secular studies advances. In science, in politics, in ethics the need is no longer felt for such a stop-gap or long-stop; he is not required in order to guarantee anything, to solve anything, or in any way to come to the rescue. In the same vein Julian Huxley writes:

The god hypothesis is no longer of any pragmatic value for the interpretation or comprehension of nature, and indeed often

[1] *Op. cit.*, pp. 145-7.

stands in the way of better and truer interpretation. Operationally, God is beginning to resemble not a ruler but the last fading smile of a cosmic Cheshire Cat.[1]

It will soon be as impossible for an intelligent, educated man or woman to believe in a god as it is now to believe that the earth is flat, that flies can be spontaneously generated, that disease is a divine punishment, or that death is always due to witchcraft. Gods will doubtless survive, sometimes under the protection of vested interests, or in the shelter of lazy minds, or as puppets used by politicians, or as refuges for unhappy and ignorant souls.[2]

And it is in this final haunt, says Bonhoeffer, that the God who has been elbowed out of every other sphere has a 'last secret place', in the private world of the individual's need. This is the sphere of 'religion' and it is here that the Churches now operate, doing their work among those who feel, or can be induced to feel, this need.

The only people left for us to light on in the way of 'religion' are a few 'last survivals of the age of chivalry', or else one or two who are intellectually dishonest. Would they be the chosen few? Is it on this dubious group and none other that we are to pounce, in fervour, pique, or indignation, in order to sell them the goods we have to offer? Are we to fall upon one or two unhappy people in their weakest moment and force upon them a sort of religious coercion?[3]

Bonhoeffer's answer is that we should boldly discard 'the religious premise', as St Paul had the courage to jettison circumcision as a precondition of the Gospel, and accept 'the world's coming of age' as a God-given fact. 'The only way to be honest is to recognize that we have to live in the world *etsi deus non daretur*[4]—even if God is not 'there'. Like children outgrowing the secure religious, moral and

[1] *Religion without Revelation*, 2nd ed., p. 58.
[2] *Op. cit.*, p. 62. Cf. S. Freud, *The Future of an Illusion* (1928), pp. 76 f.
[3] *Op. cit.*, p. 122.   [4] *Op. cit.*, p. 163.

intellectual framework of the home, in which 'Daddy' is always there in the background, 'God is teaching us that we must live as men who can get along very well without him'.[1]

The God who makes us live in this world without using him as a working hypothesis is the God before whom we are ever standing. Before God and with him we live without God. God allows himself to be edged out of the world, and that is exactly the way, the only way, in which he can be with us and help us. ... This is the decisive difference between Christianity and all religions. Man's religiosity makes him look in his distress to the power of God in the world; he uses God as a *Deus ex machina*. The Bible however directs him to the powerlessness and suffering of God; only a suffering God can help. To this extent we may say that the process we have described by which the world came of age was an abandonment of a false conception of God, and a clearing of the decks for the God of the Bible, who conquers power and space in the world by his weakness. This must be the starting point for our 'worldly' interpretation.[2]

Transcendence for Modern Man

Bonhoeffer here touches on what he would put in the place of what he has demolished, and to this we shall return in the chapters that follow. This chapter has been concerned with 'clearing the decks' and it has inevitably therefore been destructive. I have called it 'The End of Theism?', following Tillich's lead.[3] For, as he says, theism as ordinarily understood 'has made God a heavenly, completely perfect person who resides above the world and mankind'.[4] Classical Christian theology has not in fact spoken of God as 'a person'[5] (partly because the term was already pre-empted for the

[1] *Op. cit.*, p. 164.   [2] *Ibid.*
[3] *The Courage to Be*, pp. 172-6.
[4] *Systematic Theology*, vol. i (1953), p. 271.
[5] Cf. C. C. J. Webb, *God and Personality* (1919).

three 'persons' of the Trinity), and the Church's best
theologians have not laid themselves open to such attack.
They would have been content with the essential orthodoxy
of Professor Norman Pittenger's description of God as 'the
Reality undergirding and penetrating through the whole
derived creation'.[1] Yet popular Christianity has always
posited such a supreme personality. And Julian Huxley
cannot be blamed for seeing 'humanity in general, and
religious humanity in particular', as 'habituated to thinking'
of God 'mainly in terms of an external, personal, supernatural, spiritual being'.[2] Indeed, if I understand them
aright, it is still about the existence or non-existence of such
a Being that our contemporary linguistic philosophers, for
all their sophistication, continue to do battle. 'The theist',
says I. M. Crombie, 'believes in God as a transcendent
being',[3] and G. F. Woods[4] regards R. W. Hepburn as stating
the issue 'concisely and accurately' when he writes, 'The
language of "transcendence", the thought of God as a
personal being, wholly other to man, dwelling in majesty—
this talk may well collapse into meaninglessness, in the last
analysis. And yet to sacrifice it seems at once to take one
quite outside Christianity.'[5]

[1] 'Secular Study and Christian Faith', *Theology*, lxv (February 1962),
pp. 45 f. Cf., e.g., J. W. Oman, *The Natural and the Supernatural* (1931)
and W. Temple, *Nature Man and God* (1934), especially Lectures X and
XI on 'The Transcendence of the Immanent' and 'The Immanence of
the Transcendent'.
[2] *Op. cit.*, p. 14.
[3] 'The Possibility of Theological Statements' in *Faith and Logic*
(ed. B. Mitchell; 1957), p. 73 (italics his). Cf. *New Essays in Philosophical Theology* (ed. A. G. N. Flew and A. C. MacIntyre; 1955) and
A. C. MacIntyre, 'The Logical Status of Religious Belief' in *Metaphysical Beliefs* (ed. A. C. MacIntyre; 1957). A recent Gifford lecturer,
C. A. Campbell, defines theism as belief in 'the reality of a Single,
Infinite and Eternal Spirit, Perfect in Power, Wisdom and Goodness',
On Selfhood and God (1957), p. 254.
[4] 'The Idea of the Transcendent' in *Soundings*, p. 45.
[5] *Christianity and Paradox* (1958), pp. 193 f.

It is precisely the identification of Christianity—and transcendence—with this conception of theism that I believe we must be prepared to question. Does the Gospel stand or fall with it? On the contrary, I am convinced that Tillich is right in saying that 'the protest of atheism against such a highest person is correct'.[1] And this protest, which today is made in the name of the 'meaninglessness' of any such metaphysical statement, has seemed to others a matter of much greater existential concern. And to understand them we should be prepared to see how it looks to them. Huxley contents himself with saying, 'For my own part, the sense of spiritual relief which comes from rejecting the idea of God as a supernatural being is enormous'.[2] But, earlier, men like Feuerbach and Nietzsche, whom Proudhon correctly described as 'antitheists' rather than atheists,[3] saw such a supreme Person in heaven as the great enemy of man's coming of age. This was the God they must 'kill' if man was not to continue dispossessed and kept in strings. Few Christians have been able to understand the vehemence of their revolt because for them he has not been the tyrant they portrayed, who impoverishes, enslaves and annihilates man. Indeed, for most non-Christians also he has been more of a Grandfather in heaven, a kindly Old Man who could be pushed into one corner while they got on with the business of life. But the nature of his *character* is here secondary. What is important is whether such a Being represents even a distorted image of the Christian God. Can he be rehabilitated, or is the whole conception of that sort of a God, 'up there', 'out there', or however one likes to put it, a projection, an idol, that can and should be torn down?

[1] *Op. cit.*, vol. i, p. 271.   [2] *Op. cit.*, p. 24.
[3] See H. de Lubac, *The Drama of Atheist Humanism* (1949), Ch. I.

For an answer to that question I should like to end not with a theological analysis but with a personal testimony—from John Wren-Lewis, who believes that it was just such a superstition from which he was delivered in order to become a Christian:

> I cannot emphasize too strongly that acceptance of the Christian faith became possible for me *only* because I found I did not have to go back on my wholesale rejection of the superstitious beliefs that had hitherto surrounded me. The faith I came to accept was not merely different from what I had hitherto believed Christianity to be—it was utterly opposed to it, and I still regard that sort of 'religion' as an unmitigated evil, far, far more anti-Christian than atheism. This is a truth to which I do not think religious apologists pay nearly enough attention. There is a misplaced sense of loyalty which makes many Christians feel reluctant to come out in open opposition to anything that calls itself by the same name, or uses words like 'God' and 'Christ'; even Christians who in practice dislike superstition as much as I do still often treat it as a minor aberration to be hushed up rather than a radical perversion to be denounced. For example, Christian writers whose positive views are, as far as I can judge, very similar to my own, even though they may use different language to express them, still feel constrained to produce 'refutations' of the Freudian case against religion, although in fact a very large proportion of what passes for religion in our society is exactly the sort of neurotic illness that Freud describes, and the first essential step in convincing people that Christianity can be true in spite of Freud is to assert outright that belief based on the projection-mechanisms he describes is false, however much it may say 'Lord, Lord'. It is not enough to describe such beliefs as childish or primitive, for this implies that the truth is *something* like them, even though much more 'refined' or 'enlightened', whereas in reality *nothing like* the 'God' and 'Christ' I was brought up to believe in can be true. It is not merely that the Old Man in the Sky is only a mythological symbol for the Infinite Mind behind the scenes, nor yet that this Being is benevolent rather than fearful: the truth is that this whole way

of thinking is wrong, and if such a Being did exist, he would be the very devil.[1]

That, I believe, is an exaggeration. To speak thus one is in danger, like the Psalmist, of condemning a whole generation—indeed many, many generations—of God's children. It is still the language of most of his children—and particularly his older children. There is nothing intrinsically wrong with it, any more than there was with the symbolism of a localized heaven. There will be many—and indeed most of us most of the time—for whom it presents no serious difficulties and no insuperable barriers to belief. In fact, its demolition will be the greater shock to faith and will appear to leave many people bereft and 'without God in the world'. Nevertheless, I am firmly convinced that this whole way of thinking can be the greatest obstacle to an intelligent faith—and indeed will progressively be so to all except the 'religious' few. We shall eventually be no more able to convince men of the existence of a God 'out there' whom they must call in to order their lives than persuade them to take seriously the gods of Olympus. If Christianity is to survive, let alone to recapture 'secular' man, there is no time to lose in detaching it from this scheme of thought, from this particular theology or *logos* about *theos*, and thinking hard about what we should put in its place. We may not have a name yet with which to replace 'theism': indeed, it may not prove necessary or possible to dispense with the term (hence the query in the title of this chapter). But it is urgent that we should work away at framing a conception of God and the Christian Gospel which does not depend upon that projection. And to this, very tentatively, I now turn.

But before turning to it it will be well to say at once that

---

[1] *They Became Anglicans*, pp. 168 f. Quoted by kind permission of A. R. Mowbray and Co. Ltd.

our concern will not be simply to substitute an immanent for a transcendent Deity, any more than we are implying that those who worked with the previous projection thought of him as being *only* 'out there' and denied his immanence. On the contrary, the task is to validate the idea of transcendence for modern man. But this means restating its reality in other than what Bultmann has called the 'objectivized', mythological terms which merely succeed in making nonsense of it to him. For, as Professor R. Gregor Smith has said, 'The old doctrine of transcendence is nothing more than an assertion of an outmoded view of the world'.[1] Our concern is in no way to change the Christian doctrine of God but precisely to see that it does not disappear with this outmoded view.

[1] *The New Man*, p. 108.

3

THE GROUND OF OUR BEING

A Depth at the Centre of Life

THE break with traditional thinking to which I believe we are now summoned is considerably more radical than that which enabled Christian theology to detach itself from a literal belief in a localized heaven. The translation from the God 'up there' to the God 'out there', though of liberating psychological significance, represented, as I have said, no more than a change of direction in spatial symbolism. Both conceptions presuppose fundamentally the same relationship between 'God' on the one hand and 'the world' on the other: God is a Being existing in his own right to whom the world is related in the sort of way the earth is to the sun. Whether the sun is 'above' a flat earth or 'beyond' a round one does not fundamentally affect the picture. But suppose there is no Being out there at all? Suppose, to use our analogy, the skies are empty?

Now it would again be possible to present the transposition with which we are concerned as simply a change in spatial metaphor. I quoted earlier the passage from Tillich in which he proposes replacing the images of 'height' by those of 'depth' in order to express the truth of God. And there is no doubt that this simple substitution can make much religious language suddenly appear more relevant. For we are familiar today with depth psychology, and with the idea that ultimate truth is deep or profound. Moreover, while 'spiritual wickedness in high places', and all the mythology of angelic powers which the Biblical writers associate with it, seems to the modern man a fantastic phantasmagoria, similar, equally mythological, language when used by Freud of conflicts in the unconscious appears perfectly acceptable.

And the change of symbolism has real and not merely apparent psychological significance. For the category of 'depth' has richer associations than that of height. As Tillich points out:

> 'Deep' in its spiritual use has two meanings: it means either the opposite of 'shallow', or the opposite of 'high'. Truth is deep and not shallow; suffering is depth and not height. Both the light of truth and the darkness of suffering are deep. There is a depth in God, and there is a depth out of which the psalmist cries to God.[1]

And this double meaning may explain why 'depth' seems to speak to us of concern while 'height' so often signifies unconcern. The Epicurean gods, serene in their empyrean above the cares and distractions of this world, are the epitome of 'sublime' indifference. And Browning's supreme affirmation of optimism, 'God's in his heaven: all's right with the world', strikes the modern man somewhat more cynically. For if God is 'above it all' he cannot really be involved.

Yet we are not here dealing simply with a change of symbolism, important as that may be. This is not just the old system in reverse, with a God 'down under' for a God 'up there'. When Tillich speaks of God in 'depth', he is not speaking of another Being *at all*. He is speaking of 'the infinite and inexhaustible depth and ground of all being', of our ultimate concern, of what we take seriously without reservation. And after the passage I quoted earlier[2] he goes on to make the same point in relation not only to the depths

---

[1] *The Shaking of the Foundations*, p. 60.
[2] *Op. cit.*, pp. 63 f; p. 22 above.

of our personal life but to the deepest springs of our social
and historical existence:

> The name of this infinite and inexhaustible ground of history
> is *God*. That is what the word means, and it is that to which the
> words *Kingdom of God* and *Divine Providence* point. And if
> these words do not have much meaning for you, translate them,
> and speak of the depth of history, of the ground and aim of
> our social life, and of what you take seriously without reserva-
> tion in your moral and political activities. Perhaps you should
> call this depth *hope*, simply hope. For if you find hope in the
> ground of history, you are united with the great prophets who
> were able to look into the depth of their times, who tried to
> escape it, because they could not stand the horror of their
> visions, and who yet had the strength to look to an even
> deeper level and there to discover hope.[1]

What Tillich is meaning by God is the exact opposite of
any *deus ex machina*, a supernatural Being to whom one
can turn away from the world and who can be relied upon
to intervene from without. God is not 'out there'. He is in
Bonhoeffer's words 'the "beyond" in the midst of our life',
a depth of reality reached 'not on the borders of life but at
its centre',[2] not by any flight of the alone to the alone, but,
in Kierkegaard's fine phrase, by 'a deeper immersion in
existence'. For the word 'God' denotes the ultimate depth
of all our being, the creative ground and meaning of all
our existence.

So conditioned for us is the word 'God' by associations
with *a* Being out there that Tillich warns us that to make
the necessary transposition, 'you must forget everything
traditional that you have learned about God, perhaps even
that word itself'.[3] Indeed, the line between those who believe
in God and those who do not bears little relation to their

[1] *Op. cit.*, pp. 65 f.   [2] *Op. cit.*, p. 124.
[3] *Op. cit.*, p. 64.

profession of the existence or non-existence of such a Being. It is a question, rather, of their openness to the holy, the sacred, in the unfathomable depths of even the most secular relationship. As Martin Buber puts it of the person who professedly denies God,

> When he, too, who abhors the name, and believes himself to be godless, gives his whole being to addressing the *Thou* of his life, as a *Thou* that cannot be limited by another, he addresses God.[1]

For in the conditioned he has seen and responded to the unconditional. He has touched the hem of the eternal.

The difference between the two ways of thought can perhaps best be expressed by asking what is meant by speaking of a *personal* God. Theism, as the term was understood in the previous chapter, understands by this a supreme Person, a self-existent subject of infinite goodness and power, who enters into a relationship with us comparable with that of one human personality with another. The theist is concerned to argue the existence of such a Being as the creator and most sufficient explanation of the world as we know it. Without a Person 'out there', the skies would be empty, the heavens as brass, and the world without hope or compassion.

But the way of thinking we are seeking to expound is not concerned to posit, nor, like the antitheists, to depose, such a Being at all. In fact it would not naturally use the phrase 'a personal God'; for this in itself belongs to an understanding of theology and of what theological statements are about which is alien to it. For this way of thinking, to say that 'God is personal' is to say that 'reality at its very deepest level is personal', that personality is of *ultimate* significance

---

[1] *I and Thou* (1937), p. 76; cf. Tillich, *The Protestant Era* (1951), p. 65.

in the constitution of the universe, that in personal relation-ships we touch the final meaning of existence as nowhere else. 'To predicate personality of God', says Feuerbach, 'is nothing else than to declare personality as the absolute essence'.[1] To believe in God as love means to believe that in pure personal relationship we encounter, not merely what ought to be, but what is, the deepest, veriest truth about the structure of reality. This, in face of all the evidence, is a tremendous act of faith. But it is not the feat of per-suading oneself of the existence of a super-Being beyond this world endowed with personal qualities. Belief in God is the trust, the well-nigh incredible trust, that to give ourselves to the uttermost in love is not to be confounded but to be 'accepted', that Love is the ground of our being, to which ultimately we 'come home'.

If this is true, then theological statements are not a description of 'the highest Being' but an analysis of the depths of personal relationships—or, rather, an analysis of the depths of *all* experience 'interpreted by love'. Theology, as Tillich insists, is about 'that which concerns us ultimately'.[2] A statement is 'theological' not because it relates to a particular Being called 'God', but because it asks *ultimate* questions about the meaning of existence: it asks what, at the level of *theos*, at the level of its deepest mystery, is the reality and significance of our life. A view of the world which affirms this reality and significance in personal categories is *ipso facto* making an affirmation about the *ultimacy* of personal relationships: it is saying that *God*, the final truth and reality 'deep down things', *is* love. And the specifically Christian view of the world is asserting that the

[1] *The Essence of Christianity* (Eng. tr. 1854, from the second ed. of 1843), p. 97.
[2] *Systematic Theology*, vol. i, p. 15.

final definition of this reality, from which 'nothing can
separate us', since it is the very ground of our being, is 'the
love of God in Christ Jesus our Lord'.[1]

Man and God

If statements about God are statements about the
'ultimacy' of personal relationships, then we must agree
that in a real sense Feuerbach was right in wanting to
translate 'theology' into 'anthropology'. He was concerned
to restore the divine attributes from heaven to earth, whence,
he believed, they had been filched and projected on to a
perfect Being, an imaginary Subject before whom impoverished man falls in worship. Feuerbach believed that true
religion consists in acknowledging the divinity of the
attributes, not in transferring them to an illegitimate subject
(dubbed by his Marxist disciple Bakunin 'the mirage of
God'). 'The true atheist', he wrote, 'is not the man who
denies God, the subject; it is the man for whom the attributes
of divinity, such as love, wisdom and justice, are nothing.
And denial of the subject is by no means necessarily denial
of the attributes'.[2] This is, of course, very near to the position
we have been taking; and Bultmann, in answer to a challenge
from Karl Barth, says, 'I would heartily agree: I *am* trying
to substitute anthropology for theology, for I am interpreting
theological affirmations as assertions about human life'.[3]

Yet it is also clear that we are here on very dangerous
ground. For, to Feuerbach, to say that 'theology is nothing
else than anthropology' means that 'the knowledge of God
is nothing else than a knowledge of man'.[4] And his system

---

[1] Rom. 8.39.
[2] *Op. cit.*, p. 21. I have preferred, for this quotation, the translation
in H. de Lubac, *op. cit.*, p. 11.
[3] *Kerygma and Myth*, vol. i, p. 107.   [4] *Op. cit.*, p. 206.

runs out into the deification of man, taken to its logical conclusion in the Superman of Nietzsche and Auguste Comte's Religion of Humanity.

The same ambiguity is to be found in the deeply Christian humanism of Professor John Macmurray, whose thought follows similar lines. At the beginning of his Gifford Lectures he says, 'The conception of a deity is the conception of a personal ground of all that we experience',[1] and he concludes them with a chapter, 'The Personal Universe',[2] which argues a position close to that for which we have been contending. But both in these lectures and even more in his earlier book, *The Structure of Religious Experience*, he makes statements which leave one wondering whether there is anything distinctive about religion at all. For instance, 'Religion is about fellowship and community',[3] and, 'The task of religion is the maintenance and extension of human community'.[4] The question inevitably arises, if theology is translated into anthropology, why do we any longer need the category of God? Is it not 'semantically superfluous'? Is not the result of destroying 'supranaturalism' simply to end up with naturalism, as the atheists asserted?

The dilemma can be stated in another passage of Macmurray. The question of God is the question of transcendence. It is precisely this that the location of God 'up there' or 'out there' was to express and safeguard and which its denial appears to imperil. But for Macmurray transcendence is a category that applies equally to humanity:

We are both transcendent of experience and immanent in it. This union of transcendence and immanence is ... the full fact about human personality. ... We are accustomed to find it

[1] *The Self as Agent* (1957), p. 17.
[2] *Persons in Relation* (1961), Ch. X.
[3] *The Structure of Religious Experience* (1936), p. 30 f.
[4] *Op. cit.*, p. 43.

applied in theology to God, and it is usually assumed to be a peculiar and distinguishing attribute of Deity. We see now that this is a mistake. The union of immanence and transcendence is a peculiar and defining characteristic of all personality, human or divine; but it is primarily a natural, empirical fact of common human experience. Religious reflection applies it to God as a defining characteristic of universal personality because it finds it in experience as a given fact of all finite personal experience.[1]

Macmurray here denies that transcendence is distinctively an attribute of God: he asserts it as a feature of all our experience. I believe that he is wrong in what he denies, but right in what he asserts. Contrary to what he says, our experience of God *is* distinctively and characteristically an awareness of the transcendent, the numinous, the unconditional. Yet that is a feature of *all* our experience—*in depth*. Statements about God are acknowledgements of the transcendent, unconditional element in all our relationships, and supremely in our relationships with other persons. Theological statements are indeed affirmations about human existence—but they are affirmations about the ultimate ground and depth of that existence. It is not enough to say that 'religion is about human fellowship and community', any more than one can simply reverse the Biblical statement and say that 'love *is* God'. And that, significantly, is what Feuerbach thought St John should have said.[2] But it is what the Apostle rather carefully refuses to do. He is clear that *apart from* the relationship of love there is no knowledge of God: 'He who does not love does not know God; for God is love.'[3] And conversely: 'He who abides in love abides in God, and God abides in him.'[4] But the premise of this

---

[1] *Op. cit.*, pp. 27 f.
[2] *Op. cit.*, p. 261; cf. p. 47: 'Love is God himself, and apart from it there is no God.'
[3] I John 4.8.   [4] I John 4.16.

last sentence is not, as we might logically expect, 'Love is God', but, 'God is love'.[1] The most he will say the other way round is that 'love is *of* God'.[2] It is *ek theou*: it has God as its source and ground. For it is precisely his thesis[3] that our convictions about love and its ultimacy are not projections from human love; rather, our sense of the sacredness of love derives from the fact that in this relationship as nowhere else there is disclosed and laid bare the divine Ground of all our being. And this revelation for St John finds its focus and final vindication in the fact of Jesus Christ—'the humanity of God'[4]—rather than in the divinity of Man.

To assert that '*God* is love' is to believe that in love one comes into touch with the most fundamental reality in the universe, that Being itself ultimately has this character. It is to say, with Buber, that 'Every particular *Thou* is a glimpse through to the eternal *Thou*',[5] that it is 'between man and man'[6] that we meet God, not, with Feuerbach, that 'man with man—the unity of *I* and *Thou*—is God'.[7] Nevertheless, as Bonhoeffer insists, 'God is the "beyond" *in the midst*';[8] 'The transcendent is not infinitely remote but close at hand'.[9] For the eternal *Thou* is met only *in, with and under* the finite *Thou*, whether in the encounter with other persons or in the response to the natural order.

Yet the eternal *Thou* is not to be equated with the finite *Thou*, nor God with man or nature. That is the position of

[1] *Ibid.*   [2] I John 4.7.   [3] I John 4.10, 19.
[4] The title of Karl Barth's book (1961) and of the central lecture in it (pp. 37-65). Feuerbach interestingly enough also uses the phrase 'the human nature of God' (*op. cit.*, p. 49), but as always with a subtly different twist.
[5] *I and Thou*, p. 75.
[6] *Between Man and Man* (1947), pp. 30, 203-5; cf. *I and Thou*, p. 39.
[7] *Philosophie der Zukunft*, p. 62.
[8] *Op. cit.*, p. 124 (italics mine).   [9] *Op. cit.*, p. 175.

naturalism, whether pantheistic or humanistic. And, Tillich
insists, it is necessary to push 'beyond naturalism and supranaturalism'.[1] The naturalist critique of supranaturalism is
valid. It has torn down an idol and Christianity must not
be found clinging to it. But equally Christianity must
challenge the assumption of naturalism that God is merely
a redundant name for nature or for humanity. John Wren-
Lewis observes that the naturalist critique of supranaturalism
itself points to depths, divine depths, in experience for which
it fails to account. He claims that Freud's own analysis of
religion indicates as much:

> For it is an integral part of his argument that fantasies about
> spiritual forces in the occult world are really 'projections' or
> 'displacements' of elements in our experience of personal
> relationships which we seek to avoid recognizing, but it is hard
> to see why the common projections made by the human race
> should have a numinous, transcendental character *unless there
> is something numinous and transcendental in the experience of
> personal relationships themselves.*[2]

The necessity for the name 'God' lies in the fact that our
being has depths which naturalism, whether evolutionary,
mechanical, dialectical or humanistic, cannot or will not
recognize. And the nemesis which has overtaken naturalism
in our day has revealed the peril of trying to suppress them.
As Tillich puts it,

> Our period has decided for a *secular* world. That was a great
> and much-needed decision. . . . It gave consecration and

[1] *Systematic Theology*, vol. ii, p. 5.
[2] 'The Decline of Magic in Art and Politics,' *The Critical Quarterly*,
Spring 1960, p. 18. I should add that there is much in Wren-Lewis's
writings (for instance, in his subsequent elaboration of this last sentence
or in his article 'Modern Philosophy and the Doctrine of the Trinity'
in *The Philosophical Quarterly*, vol. v (1955), pp. 214-24, which makes
me doubt whether in the last analysis he himself is not expounding the
thesis 'love is God'. At any rate he certainly does not guard himself
adequately against this interpretation.

holiness to our daily life and work. Yet it excluded those deep things for which religion stands: the feeling for the inexhaustible mystery of life, the grip of an ultimate meaning of existence, and the invincible power of an unconditional devotion. These things *cannot* be excluded. If we try to expel them in their divine images, they re-emerge in daemonic images. Now, in the old age of our secular world, we have seen the most horrible manifestations of these daemonic images; we have looked more deeply into the mystery of evil than most generations before us; we have seen the unconditional devotion of millions to a satanic image; we feel our period's sickness unto death.[1]

There are depths of revelation, intimations of eternity, judgements of the holy and the sacred, awarenesses of the unconditional, the numinous and the ecstatic, which cannot be explained in purely naturalistic categories without being reduced to something else. There is the 'Thus saith the Lord' heard by prophet, apostle and martyr for which naturalism cannot account. But neither can it discount it merely by pointing to the fact that 'the Lord' is portrayed in the Bible in highly mythological terms, as one who 'inhabits eternity' or 'walks in the garden in the cool of the evening'. The question of God is the question *whether this depth of being is a reality or an illusion*, not whether *a* Being exists beyond the bright blue sky, or anywhere else. Belief in God is a matter of 'what you take seriously without any reservation', of what for you is *ultimate* reality.

The man who acknowledges the transcendence of God is the man who *in* the conditioned relationships of life recognizes the unconditional and responds to it in unconditional personal relationship. In Tillich's words again,

To call God transcendent in this sense does not mean that one must establish a 'superworld' of divine objects. It does mean

[1] *The Shaking of the Foundations*, p. 181.

that, within itself, the finite world points beyond itself. In other words, it is self-transcendent.[1]

This, I believe, is Tillich's great contribution to theology—the reinterpretation of transcendence in a way which preserves its reality while detaching it from the projection of supranaturalism. 'The Divine, as he sees it, does not inhabit a transcendent world *above nature*; it is found in the "ecstatic" character of *this* world, as its transcendent Depth and Ground.'[2] Indeed, as a recent commentator has observed, supranaturalism for Tillich actually represents 'a loss of transcendence':

> It is the attempt to understand and express God's relation to the world by a literalization of this-worldly categories. . . . The result is a God who *exists* as *a* being, *above* the world. . . . Thus God is described as an entity within the subject-object structures of the spatial-temporal world.[3]

Or, as Tillich puts it himself:

> To criticise such a conditioning of the unconditional, even if it leads to atheistic consequences, is more religious, because it is more aware of the unconditional character of the divine, than a theism that bans God into the supranatural realm.[4]

Nevertheless, the abandonment of any idea of a God 'out there' will inevitably appear a denial of his 'otherness' and the negation of much in the Biblical assertion of what Kierkegaard called 'the infinite qualitative difference between God and man'. It will be valuable therefore to look again at what the Bible is saying about the nature of God

[1] *Systematic Theology*, vol. ii, p. 8.
[2] W. M. Horton, 'Tillich's Role in Contemporary Theology' in *The Theology of Paul Tillich* (ed. C. W. Kegley and R. W. Bretall, 1952, p. 37). In his 'Reply to Interpretation and Criticism' in the same volume, Tillich describes his own position as 'self-transcending or ecstatic naturalism' (p. 341).
[3] E. Farley, *The Transcendence of God* (1962), p. 77.
[4] *The Protestant Era*, p. 92.

and see how it can retain, and indeed regain, its deepest significance in the light of this reinterpretation.

God in the Bible

One of the most searching meditations in all literature on the meaning and presence of God is to be found in Psalm 139. Here, if anywhere, there is a sense of the utterly inescapable and surpassing wonder of God *in every direction* —above, beneath, behind and before. This Psalm is a *locus classicus* for the doctrine of the omnipotence and omniscience of God. It is from this source as much as from any other that traditional theology has constructed its picture of an all-powerful Being out there beyond us, who can do everything, who knows everything, and who watches all with unsleeping eye—a sort of celestial Big Brother. It is therefore instructive to see how a theologian of Tillich's views reinterprets such a passage.

He makes the point first of all that, though it may be difficult to avoid such concepts of a super-Being in religious thought and education, 'they are at least as dangerous as they are useful'. For

in making God an object besides other objects, the existence and nature of which are matters of argument, theology supports the escape to atheism. It encourages those who are interested in denying the threatening Witness of their existence. The first step to atheism is always a theology which drags God down to the level of doubtful things. The game of the atheist is then very easy. For he is perfectly justified in destroying such a phantom and all its ghostly qualities. And because the theoretical atheist is just in his destruction, the practical atheists (all of us) are willing to use his argument to support our own attempt to flee God.[1]

[1] *The Shaking of the Foundations*, pp. 52 f.

He then continues his profound meditation on this Psalm with the words:

Let us therefore forget these concepts, *as* concepts, and try to find their genuine meaning within our own experience. We all know that we cannot separate ourselves at any time from the world to which we belong. There is no ultimate privacy or final isolation. We are always held and comprehended by something that is greater than we are, that has a claim upon us, and that demands response from us. The most intimate motions within the depths of our souls are not completely our own. For they belong also to our friends, to mankind, to the universe, and to the Ground of all being, the aim of our life. Nothing can be hidden ultimately. It is always reflected in the mirror in which nothing can be concealed. Does anybody really believe that his most secret thoughts and desires are not manifest in the whole of being, or that the events within the darkness of his subconscious or in the isolation of his consciousness do not produce eternal repercussions? Does anybody really believe that he can escape from the responsibility for what he has done and thought in secret? Omniscience means that our mystery is manifest. Omnipresence means that our privacy is public. The centre of our whole being is involved in the centre of all being; and the centre of all being rests in the centre of our being. I do not believe that any serious man can deny that experience, no matter how he may express it. And if he has had the experience, he has also met something within him that makes him desire to escape the consequence of it. For man is not equal to his own experience; he attempts to forget it; and he knows that he *cannot* forget it.[1]

And yet the Psalmist goes on to recognize that that which he is trying to escape is nothing alien to him.

The God whom he cannot flee is the Ground of his being. And this being, his nature, soul, and body, is a work of infinite wisdom, awful and wonderful. The admiration of the Divine Wisdom overcomes the horror of the Divine Presence in this passage. It points to the friendly presence of an infinitely

[1] *Op. cit.*, pp. 53 f.

creative wisdom. . . . There is a grace in life. Otherwise we could not live.[1]

God as the ground, source and goal of our being cannot but be represented at one and the same time as removed from the shallow, sinful surface of our lives by infinite distance and depth, and yet as nearer to us than our own selves. This is the significance of the traditional categories of transcendence and immanence.

The same paradoxical relationship of our lives to the deepest ground of our being is presented in the New Testament by St Paul's language about the Spirit of God and our spirits. 'Spirit'—as opposed to 'flesh', which is life in its shallowness and superficiality—speaks of that level of being and perception where the divine depths are to be known.

> The Spirit searches everything, even the depths of God. For what person knows a man's thoughts except the spirit of the man which is in him? So also no one comprehends the thoughts of God except the Spirit of God.[2]

But, St Paul continues, it is precisely this level of comprehension which is open to Christians:

> We have received not the spirit of the world, but the Spirit which is from God, that we might understand the gifts bestowed on us by God. . . . The unspiritual man does not receive the gifts of the Spirit of God, for they are folly to him, and he is not able to understand them because they are spiritually discerned. But we have the mind of Christ.[3]

And that this 'Spirit of God' is nothing alien to us but the very ground of our own true being is brought out in a further passage, for whose proper sense it is necessary to turn to the New English Bible:

> In the same way the Spirit comes to the aid of our weakness. We do not even know how we ought to pray, but through our

[1] *Op. cit.*, pp. 54 f.   [2] I Cor. 2.10 f.   [3] I Cor. 2.12-16.

inarticulate groans the Spirit himself is pleading for us, and God who searches our inmost being knows what the Spirit means, because he pleads for God's own people in God's own way; and in everything, as we know, he cooperates for good with those who love God and are called according to his purpose.[1]

In other words, the deepest groans of suffering of which the Apostle has been speaking,[2] so far from separating us from the source of our being in the love of God are in fact pointers to it, inarticulate sighs too deep for words, which the Spirit can take up and translate into prayer, because 'the Spirit' represents the link between the depths of our individual being (however shallow) and the unfathomable abyss of all being in God. God is not outside us, yet he is profoundly transcendent.

But for the Bible 'the deep things of God' cannot be plumbed, the transcendence of God cannot be understood, simply by searching the depths of the individual soul. God, since he is Love, is encountered in his fullness only 'between man and man'. And this is the burden of the whole Prophetic tradition—that it is only in response and obedience to the neighbour that the claims of God can be met and known. This message is focused in a passage to which I constantly find myself returning in the book of Jeremiah, where the prophet is addressing Jehoiakim, the son of Josiah:

> Did not your father eat and drink and do justice and righteousness? Then it was well with him. He judged the cause of the poor and needy; then it was well. *Is not this to know me? says the Lord.*[3]

God, the unconditional, is to be found only in, with *and under* the conditioned relationships of this life: for he *is* their depth and ultimate significance.

[1] Rom. 8.26-8.　　　[2] Rom. 8.18-23.　　　[3] Jer. 22.15 f.

And this receives specifically Christian expression in the profoundly simple 'parable' of the Sheep and the Goats.[1] The only way in which Christ can be met, whether in acceptance or rejection, is through 'the least of his brethren'. The Son of Man can be known only in unconditional relationship to the son of man, to the one whose sole claim upon us is his common humanity. Whether one has 'known' God is tested by one question only, 'How deeply have you loved?'—for 'He who does not love does not know God; for God is love'.[2]

Now this links up with what Bonhoeffer was saying about a 'non-religious' understanding of God. For this ultimate and most searching question has nothing to do with 'religion'. It rests our eternal salvation upon nothing peculiarly religious. Encounter with the Son of Man is spelt out in terms of an entirely 'secular' concern for food, water supplies, housing, hospitals and prisons, just as Jeremiah had earlier defined the knowledge of God in terms of doing justice for the poor and needy. Indeed, in Macmurray's words, 'the great contribution of the Hebrew to religion was that he did away with it'.[3] A right relationship to God depended on nothing religious: in fact religion could be the greatest barrier to it.[4]

The Way of the Irreligious

Our contention has been that God is to be met not by a 'religious' turning away from the world but in unconditional concern for 'the other' *seen through to its ultimate depths*, that God is, to quote Macmurray again, the 'personal ground

[1] Matt. 25.31-46. [2] I John 4.8.
[3] Quoted by G. Macleod, *Only One Way Left*, p. 67; cf. J. Macmurray, *The Clue to History* (1938), Ch. II.
[4] E.g., Amos 5.21-5.

of all that we experience'.[1] But this means, as he says, a denial that encounter with him 'rests upon some special and extraordinary type of experience apart from which it could not arise'.[2] That there are veridical experiences of the type usually called 'mystical' or 'religious' no one would be so foolish as to deny, and a man may thank God for them as St Paul did for his visions. But the capacity for religious or mystical awareness, as for aesthetic or psychic awareness, is largely a question of natural endowment. Women, for instance, appear to be naturally more religious —and more psychic—than men. To make the knowledge of God depend upon such experiences is like making it depend on an ear for music. There are those who are tone-deaf, and there are those who would not claim to have any clearly distinguishable 'religious' experiences: Oliver Chase Quick was one of them, and he wrote one of the outstanding books on Christian doctrine of our generation.[3]

That God is the 'depth' of common non-religious experience is a point upon which John Wren-Lewis also fastens in the account of his conversion. Belief in a personal God came to him, he says, through the experience of discovering in a community 'the creative and "numinous" power' inherent in *ordinary* personal relationships. And this awareness, he believes, is open to anyone.

It is indeed one of my strongest convictions, which I insist upon as the foundation for any apologetic work I set out to do, that experience of this type is common to all human beings. . . . Prayer and mystical vision are real and important, but they cannot be the primary basis for religious conviction; this must come from *common* experience, and special experiences like prayer are only meaningful, in my view, insofar as they refer back to common experience. But it is one thing to

[1] *The Self as Agent*, p. 17.   [2] *Op. cit.*, p. 18.
[3] *Doctrines of the Creed* (1938).

say that religious propositions can be referred to the common experience of the creative character of personal relationships: it would be quite another to say that people commonly *recognize* their experience of personal relationship for what it is —an encounter with the Transcendent. Clearly they do not, or there would be no need for religious apologetics—and what was special about the group of people I met through this Anglican clergyman was that he had led them to be aware of the full religious significance of their relations with one another.[1]

In fact it began to dawn upon him what he had encountered was actually an entirely different mode of living-in-relationship from anything known in the world, a *redeemed* mode of relationship in which the special energy Blake called 'mutual forgiveness' operated in a way that made the professional 'permissiveness' of the psychotherapist's consulting-room seem a pale shadow in comparison.[2]

It was, of course, a specifically *Christian* community, manifesting what Tillich describes as the power of 'the *new* being'. But it was not for that reason any the more *religious*, based upon some new kind of esoteric or pietistic experience. It was pointing through to God as the ground of all personal relationship and all being, but insisting that a man can only know that Love as the fount and goal of his own life in so far as the alienation from the ground of his being is overcome 'in Christ'. In traditional theological terms, it was declaring that the way to 'the Father'—to acknowledgement of the 'ultimacy' of pure personal relationship—is only 'by the Son'—through the love of him in whom the human is completely open to the divine—and 'in the Spirit'—within the reconciling fellowship of the new community.

And this leads us directly into the reassessment, in this whole context, of the person and work of Christ.

[1] *They Became Anglicans*, pp. 175 f.   [2] *Op. cit.*, pp. 176 f.

4

THE MAN FOR OTHERS

Christmas and Truth

THE doctrine of the Incarnation and Divinity of Christ is on any count central to the entire Christian message and crucial therefore for any reinterpretation of it. It is also the point where resistance to reinterpretation is likely to be at its maximum and where orthodoxy has its heaviest investment in traditional categories. This is true both at the level of technical theology, where any restatement must run the gauntlet of the Chalcedonian Definition and the Athanasian Creed, and at the popular level, where one will quickly be accused of destroying the Christmas story. But if it is necessary in our thinking about God to move to a position 'beyond naturalism and supranaturalism', this is no less important in our thinking about Christ. Otherwise we shall be shut up, as we have been hitherto, to an increasingly sterile choice between the two.

Traditional Christology has worked with a frankly supranaturalist scheme. Popular religion has expressed this mythologically, professional theology metaphysically. For this way of thinking, the Incarnation means that God the Son came down to earth, and was born, lived and died within this world as a man. From 'out there' there graciously entered into the human scene one who was not 'of it' and yet who lived genuinely and completely within it. As the God-man, he united in his person the supernatural and the natural: and the problem of Christology so stated is how

Jesus can be fully God and fully man, and yet genuinely one person.

The orthodox 'answer' to this problem, as formulated in the Definition of Chalcedon,[1] is within its own terms unexceptionable—except that properly speaking it is not a solution but a statement of the problem. But as a correct statement, as 'a signpost against all heresies', it had—and has—an irreplaceable value. 'The Christological dogma saved the Church', says Tillich, 'but with very inadequate conceptual tools'.[2] To use an analogy, if one had to present the doctrine of the person of Christ as a union of oil and water, then it made the best possible attempt to do so. Or rather it made the only possible attempt, which was to insist against all efforts to 'confuse the substance' that there were two distinct natures and against all temptation to break the unity that there was but one indivisible person. It is not surprising, however, that in popular Christianity the oil and water separated, and that one or the other came to the top.

In fact, popular supranaturalistic Christology has always been dominantly docetic. That is to say, Christ only appeared to be a man or looked like a man: 'underneath' he was God.

John Wren-Lewis gives a vivid description of an extreme form of this in the working-class religion in which he was brought up.

> I have heard it said again and again that the ordinary person sees Jesus as a good man and no more. Modernist clergy hold it up as a reason why doctrines like that of the Virgin Birth will not appeal widely, while Anglo-Catholic clergy urge that the ordinary man must be taught to recognize Jesus as *more* than a good man, but both agree in their estimate of where the ordinary man stands, and I am sure they are quite wrong, even

---

[1] Drawn up at the Council of Chalcedon in 451. The text is printed in *Documents of the Christian Church*, ed. H. Bettenson (1943), p. 73.
[2] *Systematic Theology*, vol. ii, p. 161.

today. Certainly up to the Second World War, the commonest vision of Jesus was not as a human being *at all*. He was a God in human form, full of supernatural knowledge and miraculous power, very much like the Olympian gods were supposed to be when they visited the earth in disguise.[1]

But even if such a view would be indignantly repudiated by orthodox Churchmen, and however much they would insist that Jesus was 'perfect man' as well as 'perfect God', still the traditional supranaturalistic way of describing the Incarnation almost inevitably suggests that Jesus was really God almighty walking about on earth, dressed up as a man. Jesus was not a man born and bred—he was God for a limited period taking part in a charade. He looked like a man, he talked like a man, he felt like a man, but underneath he was God dressed up—like Father Christmas. However guardedly it may be stated, the traditional view leaves the impression that God took a space-trip and arrived on this planet in the form of a man. Jesus was not really one of us; but through the miracle of the Virgin Birth he contrived to be born so as to appear one of us. Really he came from outside.[2]

I am aware that this is a parody, and probably an offensive one, but I think it is perilously near the truth of what most people—and I would include myself—have been brought up to believe at Christmas time. Indeed, the very word 'incarnation' (which, of course, is not a Biblical term) almost inevitably suggests it. It conjures up the idea of a divine

[1] *They Became Anglicans*, p. 165.
[2] For a powerful protest, even within the supranaturalist scheme of thought, that Jesus belonged, through and through, to the stuff of humanity, cf. Nels F. S. Ferré, *Christ and the Christian* (1958), Ch. II. Cf. W. N. Pittenger, *Proclaiming Christ Today* (1962), p. 87: 'There is no salvation in telling men that Jesus is an "intruder" from another world, who has not really shared our condition because, as an alien, he is not in fact one of us.'

substance being plunged in flesh and coated with it like chocolate or silver plating. And if this is a crude picture, substitute for it that of the Christmas collect, which speaks of the Son of God 'taking our nature upon him', or that of Wesley's Christmas hymn, with its 'veiled in flesh the Godhead see'.

But my point is not to ask how far particular expressions, or the general trend of thought they present, verge on the limits of orthodoxy but to put the question whether the entire supranaturalistic frame of reference does not make anything but a Christological *tour de force* impossible. For as long as God and man are thought of as two 'beings', each with distinct natures, one from 'the other side' and one from 'this side', then it is impossible to create out of them more than a God-man, a divine visitant from 'out there' who chooses in every respect to live like the natives. The supranaturalist view of the Incarnation can never really rid itself of the idea of the prince who appears in the guise of a beggar. However genuinely destitute the beggar may be, he *is* a prince; and that in the end is what matters.

But suppose the whole notion of 'a God' who 'visits' the earth in the person of 'his Son' is as mythical as the prince in the fairy story? Suppose there is no realm 'out there' from which the 'Man from heaven' arrives? Suppose the Christmas myth (the invasion of 'this side' by 'the other side')—as opposed to the Christmas history (the birth of the man Jesus of Nazareth)—has to go? Are we prepared for that? Or are we to cling here to this last vestige of the mythological or metaphysical world-view as the only garb in which to clothe story with power to touch the imagination? Cannot perhaps the supranaturalist scheme survive at least as part of the 'magic' of Christmas?

Yes, indeed, it can survive—as myth. For myth has its

perfectly legitimate, and indeed profoundly important, place. The myth is there to indicate the significance of the events, the divine depth of the history. And we shall be grievously impoverished if our ears cannot tune to the angels' song or our eyes are blind to the wise men's star. But we must be able to read the nativity story without assuming that its truth depends on there being a literal interruption of the natural by the supernatural, that Jesus can only be Emmanuel—God with us—if, as it were, he came through from another world. For, as supranaturalism becomes less and less credible, to tie the action of God to such a way of thinking is to banish it for increasing numbers into the preserve of the pagan myths and thereby to sever it from any real connection with history. As Christmas becomes a pretty story, naturalism—the attempt to explain Christ, like everything else, on humanistic presuppositions—is left in possession of the field as the only alternative with any claim to the allegiance of intelligent men.

Naturalism has on the whole been remarkably favourable to Christianity in the realm of Christology. Once the 'dogma' of his deity has been put out of the way, the humanist picture of Jesus is noticeably sympathetic, especially when compared with the sharpness of its 'antitheism'. Indeed, the non-Christian secularist view of Jesus shades imperceptibly into the estimate of his person in Liberal Christianity. To do it justice, let us then take the naturalistic interpretation of Christ at its highest and most positive.

This has even been ready to use the epithet 'divine' of Jesus—in the sense that he was the most God-like man that ever lived, that what he said and did was so beautiful and so true that he must have been a revelation, indeed, the supreme revelation, of God. According to this view, the divine is simply the human raised to the power of 'x'.

As Kierkegaard put it in a devastating parody more than a hundred years ago, 'If the thing is well said, the man is a genius—and if it is unusually well said, then God said it'. And by this Jesus is put 'on the same level as all those who have no authority, on the same level as geniuses, poets and the thinkers'.[1] He is one of them, albeit the highest of them.

Unfortunately this is clearly not what the New Testament is saying of Jesus. Nor does the naturalist interpretation of Christ side with Athanasius on what he recognized to be the crucial divide. To say that Jesus had a unique experience of God, that he displayed all the qualities of God, that he was like God or that God was like him—this can never add up to saying that he was 'of one substance' with the Father. And on that line Athanasius was correct in seeing that the battle must be fought, however much one may legitimately deplore the categories in which that test of orthodoxy had to be framed.

Yet the Liberals were entirely justified in the courage with which they were prepared to abandon the supranaturalistic scaffolding by which hitherto the whole structure had been supported. That house had to collapse, and they had the faith to see that Christianity need not collapse with it. Moreover, however inadequate the Liberal theology may now appear to us, it undoubtedly helped many to hold on to their faith at a time when otherwise they might have thrown it up completely. As the supranaturalistic scheme of things became incredible, a naturalistic theology was all that stood between an entire generation and abandoning the spirit and power of Jesus altogether. And the spirit and power was able in many cases to prove itself greater than the theology. Yet equally the theology has not sufficed to

[1] 'Of the Difference between a Genius and an Apostle' (1847) in *The Present Age* (Eng. tr., 1940), pp. 146 f.

commend the spirit and power. Modern humanistic naturalism has found less and less need to speak of Jesus as in any
sense 'divine'. The belief that we are at this point and in this
person in touch with *God* has increasingly been left to the
religious minority that can still accept the old mythology
as physically or metaphysically true. This is a dangerous
situation for the Christian faith, and in no way helps to
answer Bonhoeffer's searching question: 'How can Christ
become the Lord even of those with no religion?'[1]

The Claim of the New Testament

But before we ask, with Bonhoeffer, 'What *is* Christ, for
us today?'[2], we should stop and pose the prior question of
what it is we have to reinterpret, of what in fact the New
Testament is saying. For I believe that the supranaturalist,
like the naturalist, estimate of Christ, whatever its intention,
tends to be a distortion of the Biblical truth. I do not say it
necessarily is, since the mythological-metaphysical framework can obviously provide the setting, as it has in the past,
for an entirely orthodox Christology. But in practice popular
preaching and teaching presents a supranaturalistic view of
Christ which cannot be substantiated from the New Testament. It says simply that Jesus *was* God, in such a way that
the terms 'Christ' and 'God' are interchangeable. But
nowhere in Biblical usage is this so. The New Testament
says that Jesus was the Word of God, it says that God was
in Christ, it says that Jesus is the Son of God; but it does
not say that Jesus was God, simply like that.[3]

---

[1] *Op. cit.*, pp. 122 f.   [2] *Op. cit.*, p. 122.
[3] Or, rather, not in any passages that certainly require to be interpreted in this way. Passages that *may* be so interpreted are Rom. 9.5
and Heb. 1.8. But see in each case the alternative translations in the
Revised Standard Version or the New English Bible.

What it does say is defined as succinctly and accurately as it can be in the opening verse of St John's Gospel. But we have to be equally careful about the translation. The Greek runs: *kai theos en ho logos*. The so-called Authorized Version has: 'And the Word was God.' This would indeed suggest the view that 'Jesus' and 'God' were identical and interchangeable. But in Greek this would most naturally be represented by 'God' with the article, not *theos* but *ho theos*. But, equally, St John is not saying that Jesus is a 'divine' man, in the sense with which the ancient world was familiar or in the sense in which the Liberals spoke of him. That would be *theios*. The Greek expression steers carefully between the two. It is impossible to represent it in a single English word, but the New English Bible, I believe, gets the sense pretty exactly with its rendering, 'And what God was, the Word was'. In other words, if one looked at Jesus, one saw God—for 'he who has seen me, has seen the Father'.[1] He was the complete expression, the Word, of God. Through him, as through no one else, God spoke and God acted: when one met him one was met—and saved and judged—by God. And it was to this conviction that the Apostles bore their witness. In this man, in his life, death and resurrection they had experienced God at work; and in the language of their day they confessed, like the centurion at the Cross, 'Truly this man was the Son of God'.[2] Here was more than just a man: here was a window into God at work. For 'God was in Christ reconciling the world to himself'.[3]

The essential difference comes out in the matter of Jesus' claims. We are often asked to accept Christ as divine because he claimed to be so—and the familiar argument is pressed: 'A man who goes around claiming to be God

[1] John 14.9.   [2] Mark 15.39.   [3] II Cor. 5.19.

must either be God—or else he is a madman or a charlatan (*aut deus aut malus homo*)'. And, of course, it is not easy to read the Gospel story and to dismiss Jesus as either mad or bad. Therefore, the conclusion runs, he must be God.

But I am not happy about this argument. None of the disciples in the Gospels acknowledged Jesus because he claimed to be God, and the Apostles never went out saying, 'This man claimed to be God, therefore you must believe in him'. In fact, Jesus himself said in so many words, 'If I claim anything for myself, do not believe me'. It is, indeed, an open question whether Jesus ever claimed to be the Son of God, let alone God.[1] He may have acknowledged it from the lips of others—but on his own he preferred 'the Son of Man'. In Mark 14.61 f., he is reported to reply to the question at his trial, 'Are you the Christ, the Son of the Blessed?', with the simple words, 'I am'. But in the parallel passage in Matthew[2] he gives an equivocal answer: 'The words are yours' (as he does in all the Gospels when questioned by Pilate)—and what conceivable interest would Matthew have in watering down Jesus' claim?[3] We cannot be sure what titles Jesus claimed, and we should be wise, like the Apostles, not to rest our faith on them. Their message was rather that 'God has made him both Lord and Christ, this Jesus whom you crucified'.[4] That is to say, through the Resurrection God vindicated and set his seal upon this man as the one through whom he spoke and acted

[1] Indeed, by implication he *denied* being God: 'Why do you call me good? No one is good but God alone' (Mark 10.18).
[2] Matt. 26.63 f.
[3] I believe that the original text in Mark was probably 'You have said that I am', and that Matthew has shortened this to 'You have said', while the answer in Mark has subsequently been abbreviated (and heightened) to 'I am'. See my book, *Jesus and His Coming* (1957), pp. 43-51.
[4] Acts 2.36.

in final and decisive fashion. He vested himself utterly and completely in the man Christ Jesus; in him all his fullness dwelt.[1] What God was, the Word was.

There is a paradox running through all the Gospels that Jesus makes no claims for himself in his own right and at the same time makes the most tremendous claims about what God is doing through him and uniquely through him. Men's response to him *is* men's response to God: men's rejection of him *is* men's rejection of God. And the fourth Gospel merely highlights this paradox (it does not, as is usually said, present quite a different picture of the claims of Jesus) when it combines the saying that 'the Son can do nothing of his own accord, but only what he sees the Father doing'[2] with the uncompromising assertion, 'No one comes to the Father, but by me'.[3] Jesus never claims to be God, personally: yet he always claims to bring God, completely.

This paradox[4] is the point from which our reinterpretation of Christology must start. As the summary of his ministry in the fourth Gospel, Jesus cries out and says, 'He who believes in me, believes not in me but in him who sent me. And he who sees me sees him who sent me'.[5] Jesus, that is to say, reveals God by being utterly transparent to him, precisely as he is nothing 'in himself'. And Tillich makes this the criterion of the whole Christian claim that Jesus is the final revelation of God:

> The question of the final revelation is the question of a medium of revelation which overcomes its own finite conditions by sacrificing them, and itself with them. He who is the bearer of the final revelation must surrender his finitude—not only his life but also his finite power and knowledge and perfection. In

[1] Col. 1.19.   [2] John 5.19.   [3] John 14.6.
[4] Fastened on also by D. M. Baillie, *God Was in Christ* (1948), pp. 125-32.
[5] John 12.44 f.

doing so, he affirms that he is the bearer of final revelation (the 'Son of God' in classical terms). He became completely transparent to the mystery he reveals. But, in order to be able to surrender himself completely, he must possess himself completely. And only he can possess—and therefore surrender —himself completely who is united with the ground of his being and meaning without separation and disruption. In the picture of Jesus as the Christ we have the picture of a man who possesses these qualities, a man who, therefore, can be called the medium of final revelation.[1]

And thus it comes about that it is only on the Cross that Jesus can be the bearer of the final revelation and the embodiment of God's decisive act: it is 'Christ crucified' who is 'the power of God and the wisdom of God'.[2] For it is in this ultimate surrender of self, in love 'to the uttermost',[3] that Jesus is so completely united to the Ground of his being that he can say, 'I and the Father are one. . . . The Father is in me and I am in the Father'.[4]

It is in Jesus, and Jesus alone, that there is nothing of self to be seen, but solely the ultimate, unconditional love of God. It is as he emptied himself utterly of himself that he became the carrier of 'the name which is above every name',[5] the revealer of the Father's glory[6]—for that name and that glory is simply Love. The 'kenotic' theory of Christology, based on this conception of self-emptying, is, I am persuaded, the only one that offers much hope of relating at all satisfactorily the divine and the human in Christ.[7] Yet the fatal weakness of this theory as it is stated in supranaturalist terms is that it represents Christ as stripping himself precisely of those attributes of trans-

[1] *Systematic Theology*, vol. i, p. 148.   [2] I Cor. 1.23 f.
[3] John 13.1.   [4] John 10.30, 38.   [5] Phil. 2.5-11.
[6] John 17.4 f.
[7] Cf. in particular its superb elaboration in P. T. Forsyth, *The Person and Place of Jesus Christ* (1909), pp. 313-16.

cendence which make him the revelation of God.[1] The under-lying assumption is that it is his omnipotence, his omni-science, and all that makes him 'superhuman', that must be shed in order for him to become truly man. On the contrary, it is as he empties himself not of his Godhead but of himself, of any desire to focus attention on himself, of any craving to be 'on an equality with God',[2] that he reveals God. For it is in making himself nothing, in his utter self-surrender to others in love, that he discloses and lays bare the Ground of man's being as Love.

What is Christ for Us Today?

It was some such Christology, I believe, towards which Bonhoeffer was working and of which he left such tantalizing intimations behind him. Describing the process of increasing secularization, of man's coming of age without God, as a process which Christians must *welcome*, he says, in a passage which was quoted earlier:

> God allows himself to be edged out of the world and on to the cross. God is weak and powerless in the world, and that is exactly the way, the only way, in which he can be with us and help us. Matthew 8.17 makes it crystal clear that it is not by his omnipotence that Christ helps us, but by his weakness and suffering. . . . Man's religiosity makes him look in his distress to the power of God in the world; he uses God as a *Deus ex machina*. The Bible however directs him to the powerlessness and suffering of God; only a suffering God can help.[3]

And from this he proceeds to sketch out a Christology. All he has left us is a single pregnant paragraph of notes for the 'outline for a book' he never lived to write:

[1] See the damaging criticisms of D. M. Baillie, *op. cit.*, pp. 94-8, and A. M. Ramsey, *From Gore to Temple* (1960), pp. 30-43.
[2] Phil. 2.6.   [3] *Op. cit.*, p. 164.

What do we mean by 'God'? Not in the first place an abstract belief in his omnipotence, etc. That is not a genuine experience of God, but a partial extension of the world. Encounter with Jesus Christ, implying a complete orientation of human being in the experience of Jesus as one whose only concern is for others. This concern of Jesus for others the experience of transcendence. This freedom from self, maintained to the point of death, the sole ground of his omnipotence, omniscience and ubiquity. Faith is participation in this Being of Jesus (incarnation, cross and resurrection). Our relation to God not a religious relationship to a supreme Being, absolute in power and goodness, which is a spurious conception of transcendence, but a new life for others, through participation in the Being of God. The transcendence consists not in tasks beyond our scope and power, but in the nearest *Thou*[1] at hand. God in human form, not, as in other religions, in animal form —the monstrous, chaotic, remote and terrifying—nor yet in abstract form—the absolute, metaphysical, infinite, etc.—nor yet in the Greek divine-human of autonomous man, but man existing for others, and hence the Crucified. A life based on the transcendent.[2]

Jesus is 'the man for others', the one in whom Love has completely taken over, the one who is utterly open to, and united with, the Ground of his being. And this 'life for others, through participation in the Being of God', *is* transcendence. For at this point, of love 'to the uttermost', we encounter *God*, the ultimate 'depth' of our being, the unconditional in the conditioned. This is what the New Testament means by saying that 'God was in Christ' and that 'what God was the Word was'. Because Christ was utterly and completely 'the man for others', because he *was* love, he was 'one with the Father', because 'God is love'. But for this very reason he was most entirely man, the son of man, the servant of the Lord. He was indeed 'one of us'; and the symbol of the Virgin Birth can only legitimately mean what the fourth Gospel takes it to mean (if, indeed, its description of Christians reflects that of Christ[1]), namely, that the whole of his life is a life 'born not of the will of the flesh, nor of the will of man, but of God'. He is indeed not 'of this world' but 'of love'. The source and spring of his whole being is God: his is a life conceived and sustained utterly by the Holy Ghost. But he is for that reason only the more truly 'the proper Man'. In the man Christ Jesus stands revealed, exposed at the surface level of 'flesh', the depth and ground of all our being as Love.[2] The life of God, the ultimate Word of Love in which all things cohere,[3] is bodied forth completely, unconditionally and without reserve in the life of a man—the man for others and the man for God. He is perfect man and perfect God—not as a mixture of oil and water, of natural and supernatural—but as the embodiment through obedience of 'the beyond in our midst', of the transcendence of love.

To say that in him man was completely united with the Ground of his being is to say that on this understanding there is no final difference between the person of Christ and the work of Christ, the incarnation and the at-one-ment —any more indeed than there is in the New Testament

[1] John 1.13. The plural 'were born' should be preferred to the variant reading 'was born'. But see C. K. Barrett, *The Gospel according to St John* (1955), p. 137 f.: 'The reading which refers explicitly to the birth of Jesus is to be rejected; but it remains probable that John was alluding to Jesus' birth, and declaring that the birth of Christians, being rooted in God's will alone, followed the pattern of the birth of Christ himself.'

[2] John 1.14. Such I believe is what St John is saying in the words *sarx egeneto*, not (as the later term 'incarnation' suggests) that something from outside comes into and is encased in 'flesh'. Indeed, unless it is read with supranaturalist spectacles, the Prologue requires as little 'demythologizing' as any part of the New Testament.

[3] Col. 1.17.

phrase, 'God was in Christ reconciling the world to himself'. The doctrine of the Atonement is not—as in the supra-naturalist way of thinking—a highly mythological, and often rather dubious, transaction between two parties, 'God' on the one hand and 'man' on the other, who have to be brought together, and which goes to explain, in Anselm's words, 'why God became man'. Much indeed of this mytho-logical drama—such as the ransom paid to the Devil or the notion that the Father punishes the Son in our place—is in any case a perversion of what the New Testament says. But, even when it is Christian in content, the whole schema of a supernatural Being coming down from heaven to 'save' mankind from sin, in the way that a man might put his finger into a glass of water to rescue a struggling insect, is frankly incredible to man 'come of age', who no longer believes in such a *deus ex machina*. Yet Church people continue to explain the Atonement in some such terms as this, picturing the interplay of two personified parties: 'The relationship between God and man has been broken by original sin. Man could not pull himself up by his own shoe-strings, and thus the only hope of restoration was from God's side. Yet it was from our side that things had to be put right. It appeared hopeless. But God found the answer. For in Christ he himself became man, and as man reconciled us to himself.'

This construction no doubt gives expression or projection to genuine and deep-seated realities in the existential situation—and as myth should not be thrown out. But as an objective transaction supposed to have been accomplished outside us in time and space, it speaks today to remarkably few—to fewer indeed than the Christmas myth. The contrast is in fact instructive. Most people would genuinely *like* to believe the Christmas story, but wonder whether it *can* be true with the world as it is after nearly two thousand years. But in the case of the Atonement they ask with some impatience how anything done two thousand years ago on the Cross *could* 'affect me now'. As a description of some metaphysical *opus operatum* the 'full, perfect and sufficient sacrifice, oblation, and satisfaction for the sins of the whole world' supposed to have been 'made' on Calvary requires, I believe, for most men today more demythologizing even than the Resurrection. At no point does the supranaturalist scheme appear less compelling. And yet at no point is the naturalistic view, even in its Liberal Christian form, shallower or more discredited than in its estimate of what is wrong with the world and of what is required to put it right. The case for pushing beyond them both to a third alternative is very urgent.

In seeking for this third alternative, let us begin by listening once again to Tillich, as he speaks of the state of our human condition. For I believe his words have the power to speak universally, even to those with no sense of religion or of any God 'out there' who might be called upon to intervene.

> The state of our whole life is estrangement from others and ourselves, because we are estranged from the Ground of our being, because we are estranged from the origin and aim of our life. And we do not know where we have come from, or where we are going. We are separated from the mystery, the depth, and the greatness of our existence. We hear the voice of that depth; but our ears are closed. We feel that something radical, total, and unconditioned is demanded of us; but we rebel against it, try to escape its urgency, and will not accept its promise.
>
> We cannot escape, however. If that something is the Ground of our being, we are bound to it for all eternity, just as we are bound to ourselves and to all other life. We always remain in the power of that from which we are estranged. That fact

brings us to the ultimate depth of sin: separated and yet bound, estranged and yet belonging, destroyed and yet preserved, the state which is called despair. Despair means that there is no escape. Despair is 'the sickness unto death'. But the terrible thing about the sickness of despair is that we cannot be released, not even through open or hidden suicide. For we all know that we are bound eternally and inescapably to the Ground of our being. The abyss of separation is not always visible. But it has become more visible to our generation than to the preceding generations, because of our feeling of meaninglessness, emptiness, doubt, and cynicism—all expressions of despair, of our separation from the roots and the meaning of our life. Sin in its most profound sense, sin as despair, abounds amongst us.[1]

It is this union-in-estrangement with the Ground of our being—what Paul Althaus once described as 'inescapable godlessness in inescapable relationship to God'[2]—that we mean by hell. But equally it is the union-in-love with the Ground of our being, such as we see in Jesus Christ, that is the meaning of heaven. And it is the offer of that life, in all its divine depth, to overcome the estrangement and alienation of existence as we know it that the New Testament speaks of as the 'new creation'. This new reality is trans-cendent, it is 'beyond' us, in the sense that it is not ours to command. Yet we experience it, like the Prodigal, as we 'come to ourselves'. For it is a coming home, or rather a being received home, to everything we are created to be. It is what the New Testament can only call *grace*. And in the same sermon Tillich speaks of it in a way that shows how little it can be contained within any purely naturalistic categories, and yet how it is 'nearer to us than we are ourselves': for it is *our* 'new being'. Yet we cannot will it:

It happens; or it does not happen. And certainly it does *not*

[1] *The Shaking of the Foundations*, pp. 161 f.
[2] *Die letzten Dinge* (4th ed., 1933), p. 183.

happen if we try to force it upon ourselves, just as it shall not
happen so long as we think, in our self-complacency, that we
have no need of it. Grace strikes us when we are in great pain
and restlessness. It strikes us when we walk through the dark
valley of a meaningless and empty life. It strikes us when we
feel that our separation is deeper than usual, because we have
violated another life, a life which we loved, or from which we
were estranged. It strikes us when our disgust for our own
being, our indifference, our weakness, our hostility, and our
lack of direction and composure have become intolerable to us.
It strikes us when, year after year, the longed-for perfection
of life does not appear, when the old compulsions reign within
us as they have for decades, when despair destroys all joy and
courage. Sometimes at that moment a wave of light breaks into
our darkness, and it is as though a voice were saying: 'You are
accepted. *You are accepted*, accepted by that which is greater
than you, and the name of which you do not know. Do not
ask for the name now; perhaps you will find it later. Do not
try to do anything now; perhaps later you will do much. Do
not seek for anything; do not perform anything; do not
intend anything. *Simply accept the fact that you are accepted!*'
If that happens to us, we experience grace. After such an
experience we may not be better than before, and we may not
believe more than before. But everything is transformed. In
that moment, grace conquers sin, and reconciliation bridges
the gulf of estrangement. And nothing is demanded of this
experience, no religious or moral or intellectual presupposition,
nothing but *acceptance*.

In the light of this grace we perceive the power of grace in our
relation to others and to ourselves. We experience the grace of
being able to look frankly into the eyes of another, the
miraculous grace of reunion of life with life. We experience the
grace of understanding each other's words. We understand
not merely the literal meaning of the words, but also that which
lies behind them, even when they are harsh or angry. For even
then there is a longing to break through the walls of separation. We experience the grace of being able to accept the life
of another, even if it be hostile and harmful to us, for, through
grace, we know that it belongs to the same Ground to which
we belong, and by which we have been accepted. We experience

the grace which is able to overcome the tragic separation of the sexes, of the generations, of the nations, of the races, and even the utter strangeness between man and nature. Sometimes grace appears in all these separations to reunite us with those to whom we belong. For life belongs to life.[1]

In all this we can recognize what St Paul is saying of the new creation or the new man 'in Christ Jesus'. It is nothing peculiarly religious—it is 'neither circumcision nor uncircumcision'.[2] It is the life of 'the man for others', the love whereby we are brought completely into one with the Ground of our being, manifesting itself in the unreconciled relationships of our existence. It was manifested supremely on the Cross, but it is met wherever the Christ is shown forth and recognized in 'an entirely different mode of living-in-relationship from anything known in the world'.[3] For there, in however 'secular' a form, is the atonement and the resurrection. And the Christian community exists, not to promote a new religion, but simply to be the embodiment of this new being as love. And that means, to return in closing to Bonhoeffer, 'participation in the powerlessness of God in the world'.[4]

> Christians range themselves with God in his suffering; that is what distinguishes them from the heathen. As Jesus asked in Gethsemane, 'Could ye not watch with me one hour?' That is the exact opposite of what the religious man expects from God. Man is challenged to participate in the sufferings of God at the hands of a godless world.
>
> He must therefore plunge himself into the life of a godless world, without attempting to gloss over its ungodliness with a veneer of religion or trying to transfigure it. He must live a 'worldly' life and so participate in the suffering of God. He

---

[1] Op. cit., pp. 163 f.
[2] Gal. 6.15. See the notable sermon on this text by Tillich that gives its title to his other collection, The New Being (1956), pp. 15-24.
[3] J. Wren-Lewis, quoted above, p. 63.   [4] Op. cit., p. 167.

may live a worldly life as one emancipated from all false religions and obligations. To be a Christian does not mean to be religious in a particular way, to cultivate some particular form of asceticism (as a sinner, a penitent or a saint), but to be a man. It is not some religious act which makes a Christian what he is, but participation in the suffering of God in the life of the world.[1]

But to take that last sentence seriously compels us to weigh the consequences of so radical a challenge to region-less Christianity. What can it mean for a man's membership of the Christian society, and for the 'religious acts' which play such a large part in it?

[1] *Op. cit.*, p. 166.

5

WORLDLY HOLINESS

The Holy in the Common

'WHAT is the place of worship and prayer in an entire absence of religion?' Bonhoeffer's question,[1] which he never survived to answer, may sound too paradoxical to be intelligible. For worship and prayer would seem to be *the* expression of religion, the activities *par excellence* that distinguish a religious person from an irreligious. But we dare not simply dismiss the question. Rather, let it drive us to a more careful definition of terms.

Perhaps the best way to define 'religious' would be to ask, for instance, what is the difference between a religious film and a Christian film. Most people would without thinking tend to equate the two. But clearly there is an important distinction to be made. A Christian film is one that embodies Christian judgements on situations, Christian valuations of personal relationships, Christian insights into the purpose and meaning of life. A religious film is one that is about a certain area of experience or activity. It could have a Biblical or quasi-biblical subject, it could be about nuns, or Lourdes, or centre round some religious movement or experience. It is possible for the former category to have nothing specifically to do with religion at all, while the latter, as we know, can be nauseatingly and profoundly unchristian.

The 'religious', in the technical sense of the religious orders, is the antithesis of the 'secular'. It relates to that

[1] *Op. cit.*, p. 123.

department of life which is contrasted with 'the world'; and in its popular non-technical sense it includes all those activities which go on within the circle of the sanctuary, whether literally or metaphorically. It is a particular area of experience or activity into which a man may turn aside or 'go apart', and which has its own psychology and sociology. A 'religious revival' means the burgeoning of this area of experience and activity, and the process of secularization its diminution or decline. And the Churches are universally assumed to have a vested interest in the former and to deplore the latter.

It is this assumption against which Bonhoeffer is putting his question mark. Does this mean he does not want anyone to go to Church or say his prayers? Evidently not.[1] For otherwise he would not ask what was the place of worship and prayer in the absence of religion. For they would obviously have no place. How then should we answer his question? Let us ask it in turn, as he does, first of worship—public prayer, liturgy, the cultus—and then of private prayer—personal devotion, piety, and 'the spiritual life'.

Liturgy and worship would, on the face of it, seem to be concerned essentially with what takes place in a consecrated building, with the holy rather than the common, with 'religion' rather than 'life'. They belong to, and indeed virtually constitute, that area or department of experience which appeals to 'the religious type', to those who 'like that sort of thing' or 'get something out of it'. Worship

[1] This is the point above all where Bonhoeffer's mind cannot be understood without also taking into account his previous writings, especially *Life Together* (1954). Nevertheless, the answer to his question is *not* to be found in the piety of the earlier period. Rather, as Martin E. Marty says in his introduction to R. H. Fuller's article, 'Liturgy and Devotion', in *The Place of Bonhoeffer*, pp. 167-96, the two stages must be seen in polarity and dialectical relationship: 'The Church inhales and exhales.'

and church-going except as an expression of an interest in religion would not seem to most people to be meaningful.

And yet the sacrament which forms the heart of Christian worship is the standing denial of all this. It is the assertion of 'the "beyond" *in the midst of our life*', the holy *in* the common. The Holy Communion is *the* point at which the common, the communal, becomes the carrier of the unconditional, as the Christ makes himself known in the breaking and sharing of bread. *Holy* Communion is communion, community-life, *in sacris*, in depth, at the level at which we are not merely in human fellowship but 'in Christ', not merely in love but in Love, united with the ground and restorer of our whole being. At least that is what Communion should be. But too often it is not the place at which the common and the communal point through to the beyond in their midst, to the transcendent in, with and under them, but precisely the opposite.[1] It ceases to be the holy meal, and becomes a religious service in which we turn our backs on the common and the community and in individualistic devotion go to 'make our communion' with 'the God out there'. This is the essence of the religious perversion,[2] when worship becomes a realm into which to withdraw from the world to 'be with God'—even if it is only in order to receive

---

[1] Cf. the following from a (nameless) parish magazine in my diocese: 'Christians today withdraw from the world by attendance at the service of Holy Communion. Our Lord commanded us to do this. During 1961, 12,526 Communions were received, being an increase of over 500 from the previous year.'

[2] This is perhaps the point to recognize that so much of the discussion for and against 'religion' is bound to be a matter of definition. Ultimately I believe that Tillich is right in saying that 'Religion is not a special function of man's spiritual life, but it is the dimension of depth in all of its functions'. What he admits is 'the narrower and customary sense of the word' is a result of the estrangement of sin (*Theology of Culture*, 1959, pp. 5 f.; cf. *The Protestant Era*, pp. 65 f.). But I have preferred to retain the customary usage in order to bring out the point of Bonhoeffer's critique.

strength to go back into it. In this case the entire realm of the non-religious (in other words, 'life') is relegated to the profane, in the strict sense of that which is outside the *fanum* or sanctuary. The holy place, where the Christ is met, lies not, as in the parable of the Sheep and the Goats, in the ordinary relationships of life: it lies within the circle of 'the religious', from which the worshipper will go out to carry Christ's love into 'the secular world'. Worship, liturgy, on this understanding, is not meeting the holy *in* the common. The holy is that which is not common and which has to be taken from the temple in order to sanctify the common. The sphere of the religious constitutes the holy of holies, and we are back at the Jewish priestly conception of the relation of the sacred to the secular which was shattered by the Incarnation when God declared all things holy and the veil of the temple was rent from top to bottom.

For Christianity, on the other hand, the holy is the 'depth' of the common, just as the 'secular' is not a (godless) section of life but the world (God's world, for which Christ died) cut off and alienated from its true depth. The purpose of worship is not to retire from the secular into the department of the religious, let alone to escape from 'this world' into 'the other world', but to open oneself to the meeting of the Christ in the common, to that which has the power to penetrate its superficiality and redeem it from its alienation. The function of worship is to make us more sensitive to these depths; to focus, sharpen and deepen our response to the world and to other people beyond the point of proximate concern (of liking, self-interest, limited commitment, etc.) to that of ultimate concern; to purify and correct our loves in the light of Christ's love; and in him to find the grace and power to be the reconciled and reconciling community. Anything that achieves this or assists towards it is Christian worship. Anything that fails to do this is not Christian worship, be it ever so 'religious'.

All this finds its focus, as I have already indicated, in *the* liturgy that forms the heart of Christian worship. Liturgy (a word which comes in origin from the world not of the cultus but of 'public works') is not for the Christian a 'religious' rite but the proclamation, the acknowledgement, the reception, the adoration, of the holy in, with and under the common. The bread and the wine that stand at the heart of the action and form its basis are samples only of all other common things and the focus of all other common relationships. The Holy Communion is the proclamation to the Church and to the world that the presence of Christ with his people is tied to a right receiving of the common, to a right relationship with one's neighbour. For it is given only in and through these things, both in church and out of it. What the action in church does is to set forth this truth in symbol and in power. And therefore the pattern of this action is formative for the whole of Christian living. It must be made to represent the truth that 'the beyond' is to be found 'at the centre of life', 'between man and man'. That is why the Prayer Book indicates that the bread to be used for Communion shall be 'such as is usual to be eaten'; that is why the deepest insights into the meaning of 'God's board' have come for many in our generation not in the 'glass case' of the sanctuary but at their own hearth; that is why the liturgical revival has expressed itself in the recovery of the central altar with the celebration *by* the whole people gathered *round* the table.[1]

----

[1] I have deliberately not gone into details at this point, because I have already written extensively on it in my *Liturgy Coming to Life* (1960).

Indeed, the very difference of position at the Communion table, so trivial a thing and apparently so ritualistic and removed from life, is in itself symbolic of much of what we have been trying to say. The so-called 'eastward position', in which the priest stands with his back to the people, has the psychological effect of focusing attention upon a point somewhere in the middle distance beyond the sanctuary. It symbolizes the whole way of thinking in which God is seen as a projection 'out there' to whom we turn from the world. By contrast the 'westward position', in which the president surrounded by his assistants faces the people across the table, focuses attention upon a point in the middle, as the Christ stands among his own as the breaker of bread. There is equally here—or should be—the element of 'the beyond', the transcendent, as they lift their hearts to him as their ascended and triumphant Lord. But the beyond is seen not as that which takes one out and away from the earthly and the common, but as the vertical of the uncon- ditioned cutting into and across the limitations of the merely human fellowship, claiming it for and transforming it into the Body of the living Christ. Moreover, the whole tendency connected with this transition of thought and expression is to strip away the associations of churchiness and religiosity and everything that sets apart the sanctuary from society, and to let the décor, the music and the architecture speak the language of the world it is meant to be transforming.

Such at any rate is the *direction* in which, I believe, we should begin to look for the answer to Bonhoeffer's question about the meaning of worship in the absence of religion— though we have a very, very long way to go, and churchiness will keep on reasserting itself.

Liturgy, however reformed, can so easily simply create 'another world' of its own, a world where everything is 'done' according to the latest (or the oldest) models and which yet merely goes on side by side with real life. As Eric James puts it,

> These actions will have an independent life of their own, an ecclesiastical life; something which belongs to the Church for its own sake; something which is neither natural nor necessarily supernatural. . . . The great danger is that liturgy creates a world of things over against the secular, instead of a vision of the sacredness of the secular.[1]

The test of worship is how far it makes us *more sensitive* to 'the beyond in our midst', to the Christ in the hungry, the naked, the homeless and the prisoner. Only if we are *more likely* to recognize him there after attending an act of worship is that worship Christian rather than a piece of religiosity in Christian dress. That is what is implied in Jesus' saying that 'the sabbath was made for man, not man for the sabbath'.[2] The whole of our religious observance and church-going must be prepared to submit to its test. And we should have the courage to draw the consequences, as John Wren-Lewis has done in an article entitled, 'On Not Going to Church':[3]

> If the general atmosphere prevailing in a particular church is one which reverses the order of Jesus' statement, and conveys the sense that people actually go to church to *find* God, to enter into a relationship with him which is not possible apart from specific acts of worship, then it would be a miracle if you *did* get the right thing out of going to such a church, and one has no business tempting God by asking for miracles. It is *much* better to stay away. Perhaps the ideal would be to try to revolutionize the church in question, by bringing its members to see the plain meaning of their own Gospel, but some kinds of church tradition are heavily protected against this, and one

[1] *The Roots of the Liturgy*, *Prism* Pamphlet No. 1 (1962), p. 5.
[2] Mark 2.27.   [3] *Prism*, February 1962, p. 28.

must have a realistic assessment of one's revolutionary capacities.

That no doubt is a hard saying, especially for parsons; but no harder than Jesus' original saying was to the rabbis. It did not mean the end of church-going for him and it does not mean it for us. But it meant for Judaism a revolution in its whole conception of holiness—or its decline and fall.

Perhaps it would be fairer to say not that this conception of worship is in itself of 'the very devil' but that it belongs to a way of thinking which can indeed still inspire the 'religious' to genuine Christian living, but which for the rest merely removes 'the beyond' from their midst and sets God further away. And, unless—against all the protests of the religious—the Church can discover and stand for a different conception of worship 'in an entire absence of religion', it too is set for decline and fall.

Engagement and Disengagement

This sense which Dr Wren-Lewis describes (and which marks the essential divide), that a person goes to church to *find* God, to enter into a relationsip with him which is not possible in 'the world', is one that is equally pervasive when we turn from public worship to private prayer. Prayer is conceived in terms of turning aside from the business of 'the world' to 'be with God'. However much the various methods and techniques of prayer may differ, they all tend to start from the assumption that prayer is to be *defined* in terms of what one does in the times of *dis*engagement. Of course, they all go on to insist that this activity must then permeate and irrigate the whole of life. But the sacramental moments of communion with God are to be expected in the periods of withdrawal, which, like the camel's water, are to see one through the deserts of the day that must otherwise drain one dry. And even 'arrow prayers' in the midst of the hurly burly presuppose an ejaculation, however momentary, *from* the pressures of the world *to* a God out there and above them all, with whom we can still hold communion *in spite of* them.

This is readily recognizable as another version of trying to 'find God in the gaps'. And in modern life, as in modern science, the gaps get smaller and smaller.

> The world is too much with us; late and soon,
> Getting and spending, we lay waste our powers.

That we all admit. Concentration is ravaged: the spaces dwindle to vanishing point, and we are consumed. What do we do?

The traditional answer has been to retain the basic presupposition but to do our best to redeem the time. Our traditional forms of spirituality have been adapted from the monasteries for the millions. The assumption is that the heart of prayer is withdrawal. Obviously not everyone has the time in a busy life for much withdrawal, nor has everyone the proficiency for it. Therefore, it is right that there should be special men and women whose life and ministry this is. These are 'the religious', whose pattern of spirituality provides the norm. This pattern is found in its purest form in the contemplative orders, but it can be adapted to different degrees of life in the world for the other religious communities, the 'secular' clergy, and finally by much dilution for 'the laity'. By this stage the gaps may have shrunk considerably, but even the layman can be exhorted and expected to set aside regular 'spaces' for prayer and to make an annual 'retreat'.

The last thing I want to do is to caricature this approach

or to deny its profound value for those who can benefit from it. Nor, as will appear, do I wish in any way to doubt the virtue, and indeed the absolute necessity, for withdrawal, disengagement, standing back. Nor, of course, should I be so foolish as to dispute the need in this field, as in every other, for experts; and it will become painfully obvious that I am not one. Nevertheless, I believe that some things need to be said on behalf of those who are not experts and who suffer for lack of a spokesman. And I speak with some feeling. For I believe the experts have induced in us a deep inferiority complex. They tell us that this is the way we ought to pray, and yet we find that we cannot maintain ourselves for any length of time even on the lowest rungs of the ladder, let alone climb it. If this is the *scala sacra*, then it seems it is not for us. We are evidently not 'the praying type'. And so we carry on with an unacknowledged sense of failure and guilt.

I can testify to this most strongly from the time I spent in a theological college, both as a student and as a teacher. Here was a laboratory for prayer. Here one ought to be able to pray, if ever one could. For here were all the conditions laid on—time, space, quiet. And here were the teachers, the classics of the spiritual life, and all the aids and manuals. If one failed in these circumstances what hope was there later on—when one was surrounded and sucked down by 'the world'? And yet I believe I am not alone in finding a theological college the most difficult rather than the easiest of places in which to pray. In fact I know I am not. For I discovered there what I can only describe as a freemasonry of silent, profoundly discouraged, underground opposition, which felt that all that was said and written about prayer was doubtless unexceptionable but simply did not speak to 'our' condition. It was a real relief finding kindred spirits and slowly coming to the conviction from shared confession that we might not after all, as the evidence suggested, represent merely an 'unclubbable' remnant for whom not even the outer rooms seemed designed to cater. But nothing else was offered in its place, and to this day we have an inferiority complex. We dare not admit to others or to ourselves what non-starters we are. And yet I am persuaded that we have 'got something', and though, like the people in Chesterton's poem, we 'have not spoken yet', nevertheless our hour may be at hand. For one can detect a ground swell of dissatisfaction, and a murmuring for something more relevant in the way of what is styled a 'lay spirituality'.

But though we can all understand what is meant by such a phrase, I question whether it puts the distinction in the right place—on the assumption that 'lay' here means 'non-ordained'. Though there may be a difference of kind between the spirituality appropriate to the 'religious' (in the technical sense) and to the Christian set in the world (whether as a priest or as a layman), I am not convinced that there is more than a difference of degree between the 'secular' spirituality which is appropriate to the clergy and to the laity. I believe the yearning which is felt for something more 'earthed' reflects a more general discontent with the traditional types of spirituality and that we clergy cover up the uncomfortable knowledge that they have long been failing us, and that we have failed to communicate a relevant spirituality to our people, by saying that what we need is something new for 'the laity'.

The only writing on prayer I know which has the courage to ask whether we do not need an entirely new starting point is the chapter in George Macleod's prophetic book, *Only One Way Left*. It is significant that this is entitled, 'The

Prayer Life of a Christian Minister in a Committed Church'.
It is not only for laymen, it is for the *Laos*, but for the *Laos*
in the mid-twentieth century. Dr Macleod makes something
of the same point as Bonhoeffer when he says that our
greatest difficulty is '*our difference from medieval man*, when
so many of our "aids to prayer" stem from a medieval
pattern'. And he goes on:

> I have what I call 'bankrupt corner' in my library and I am, if
> negatively, encouraged to discover it on the manse shelves of
> most ministers who have tried to pray. It is a platoon of ban-
> tam booklets enlisted at intervals to help one to pray better:
> purchased, as each severally went dead on us, on the principle
> that 'Hope springs eternal'. Why do they go dead on us?
> Because most of them are written in terms of a different
> consciousness. Because most of them are conceived in medieval
> terms, we are not really conditioned to read what they are
> really saying. For medieval man life was dull, brutish and
> short. Life here was over against the real life of the Spirit. . . .
> We moderns are of a different expectancy to medieval man.
> Life is not brutish or short. We are girt about with possibilities.
> If medieval man looked up through a telescope, we rather look
> down through a microscope. Matter is so marvellous. If his
> fears were ghosts in the heavenlies, ours are in the infinitesimal
> but infernal and paradoxically infinite possibilities of hydrogen.
> . . . Modern man is earthed; materially environed. His devo-
> tions are transmuted. There is no advance in all this. We are
> enmeshed in this materialism. But the secret of our exit is of
> vast importance.[1]

What is 'the secret of our exit'? He describes the exit
taken by the spiritually minded as 'the world' closed in
upon them with the secularization of the Church under
Constantine. That exit led them into the sands of Egypt.
'They introduced the Via Negativa: the way of interior
denial. Unfortunately the Via Negativa cuts dead across the
Emmaus Road.'[2] Yet the *via negativa* underlay the whole

[1] *Op. cit.*, pp. 151 f.   [2] *Op. cit.*, p. 152.

medieval 'way of perfection' which defined the various stages of prayer (purgative, illuminative, unitive) in 'the ladder of ascent'. Dr Macleod has the courage to question whether such is 'even the royal road to holiness within the Christian dispensation'. It is not merely a matter, as we have already suggested, of 'how many earthbound mortals have departed almost completely from a serious prayer-life because they thought such the essence of prayer, and are benumbed by their failure to attain it.[1] His real doubt is the capacity of such a type of prayer to keep men on what he calls 'the knife-edge' between pietism on the one hand and the slide into materialism on the other. 'So delectable, if demanding, is the exercise' of such prayer of interior denial that

> they are apt to cut off the telephone when a whole world is trying to get through to them in the extremity of our need. None the less, it is these whom we are inclined to suppose are the truly religious, or the really spiritual.
> Alternatively, the rest of us, feeling we are not made for it, embrace the practical and slither on to the knife-edge walk without sufficient prayer. We dismiss the bantam platoon, so constant now is the telephone. We comparably degenerate just at the moment when, if we seriously recovered the pristine holiness, we might have the word for our world.
> There remain the cross-benchers who become hardly dependable for either school. Now practical, now spiritual, their telephone just ceases to ring. Neither to conduct a retreat or lead a 'war on want' are they fitted.
> We are immersed in the here and now. We know we must be. But too often when we turn to prayer the isolation intensifies, the medieval resurrects and neither life becomes powerful nor prayer real.[2]

Where in this situation do we turn? It is the same question, fundamentally, that Bonhoeffer was asking. And

[1] *Op. cit.*, p. 153.   [2] *Op. cit.*, p. 153 f.

the answer, I believe, is in the direction he indicated. I suspect we have got to ask very seriously whether we should even begin our thinking about prayer in terms of the times we 'set aside', whether prayer is primarily something we do in the 'spaces', in the moments of disengagement from the world. I wonder whether Christian prayer, prayer in the light of the Incarnation, is not to be *defined* in terms of penetration through the world to God rather than of withdrawal from the world to God. For the moment of revelation is precisely so often, in my experience, the moment of meeting and unconditional *engagement*. How easily one finds oneself giving pious advice to a person faced with a decision to 'go away and pray about it'. But, if I am honest, what enlightenment I have had on decisions has almost always come not when I have gone away and stood back from them, but precisely as I have *wrestled through* all the most practical pros and cons, usually with other people. And this activity, undertaken by a Christian trusting and expecting that God is there, would seem to *be* prayer.

This can perhaps be put another way by saying that traditional spirituality has placed a premium upon 'the interior life', regarding this as the spiritual core of man. But Bonhoeffer points out that the Bible knows nothing of such a premium: 'The "heart" in the biblical sense is not the inward life, but the whole man in relation to God.'[1] And he goes on to make the telling remark that for the Bible 'man lives just as much from outwards to inwards as from inwards to outwards'.[2] This I believe to be profoundly true for great numbers of people, probably for the majority. For them 'real life is meeting'.[3] They are, of course, subject to the rhythm of engagement and disengagement, just as

[1] *Op. cit.*, p. 160; cf. p. 126. [2] *Ibid.*
[3] The title of a book by J. H. Oldham (1942).

the capacity of the body to function creatively depends upon the quality of its relaxation. Nevertheless, in so far as an assessment is made of our physical capacity and alertness, it is made on the evidence of our waking hours. And for such people, 'their prayer is in the practice of their trade'.[1] The need for times of withdrawal is accepted naturally, but with no pretension that these times are particularly 'holy': nor will they necessarily be more 'religious', in the sense that they are devoted to spiritual exercises. They are basically times of standing back, of consolidation, of letting love's roots grow. And these may be fertilized by many different processes of action or inaction.

I should be the last to say that periods of disengagement are not absolutely vital. In fact I have only been able to write this because of one such period. And this may be allowed to serve as an illustration of how, as it seems to me, they should be related to life. I am one of those who find that all my thinking and writing comes to me through immersion in what I have to *do*. Indeed, it is largely only literally by the activity of writing, with pen in hand, that I can think at all. And without the constant stimulus of problems to be solved, persons to be helped, pupils to be taught, nothing comes to the surface. Isolate myself from the world, and there is no grist to the mill. But it is equally clear that it is not only the mills of God that grind slowly. Time, space, withdrawal, if only from the telephone, is necessary if any fruit is to be brought to perfection.

I find that this is a paradigm also for prayer. It is certainly not that disengagement is unnecessary, but that the pentecostal point, as it were, is in the engagement. To try to clarify the difference, let me speak as a fool in contrast for a moment with my uncle Forbes Robinson, whose *Letters*

[1] Ecclus. 38.34.

to his Friends[1] so vividly show a 'lay spirituality' really being communicated. Forbes would constantly say, 'I am seeing so-and-so; I must put aside an hour first to pray for him', or even, 'I could help him more if I set apart the hour in which I would have seen him to pray for him'. This, I find, just doesn't work out in practice; and I am not convinced that it is *merely* due to my incomparably dimmer candle-power. My own experience is that I am really praying for people, agonizing with God for them, precisely *as* I meet them and really give my soul to them. It is then if ever, in this incarnational relationship, that deep speaks to deep and the Spirit of God is able to take up our inarticulate groans and turn them into prayer. It is *afterwards* that I find one needs to withdraw—as it were, to clarify on tablets and bring to obedience the revelation given on the mount.

A 'Non-religious' Understanding of Prayer

Perhaps this is the starting point for a 'non-religious' understanding of prayer. We may begin from the fact that people do give themselves to people. There is nothing 'religious' about this. But to open oneself to another *unconditionally* in love *is* to be with him in the presence of God, and that is the heart of intercession. To pray for another is to expose both oneself and him to the common ground of our being; it is to see one's concern for him in terms of *ultimate* concern, to let *God* into the relationship. Intercession is to *be with* another at that depth, whether in silence or compassion or action. It may consist simply in listening, when we take the otherness of the other person most seriously.[2] It may not be talking *to* God, as though

[1] Recently re-edited by M. R. J. Manktelow under the title *Forbes Robinson: Disciple of Love* (1961).
[2] See Bonhoeffer, *Life Together*, pp. 87-9.

to a third person, about him at all. The *Thou* addressed may be his own *Thou*, but it may be addressed and responded to at such a level that we can only speak of knowing him in God and God in him. It may not be specifically religious, it may not be consciously Christian: but it may be a meeting of Christ in that man, because his humanity is accepted 'without any reservation'. The way through to the vision of the Son of man and the knowledge of God, which is the heart of contemplative prayer, is by unconditional love of the neighbour, of 'the nearest *Thou* to hand'.

Prayer is the responsibility to meet others with *all* I have, to be ready to encounter the unconditional in the conditional, to expect to meet God in the way, not to turn aside from the way. All else is exercise towards that or reflection in depth upon it. It was on the Damascus road that Saul had his encounter with Christ: he was driven to Arabia by it. He did not have to go to Arabia to seek God; but equally from Arabia he returned deepened in the power of the Spirit. There is an inescapable dialectic of engagement and withdrawal. But much depends on which we regard as primary. There is no sense in which a Christian *has* to turn aside from the world in order to meet God—any more than the holy of holies is for him in the sanctuary. But there is a sense in which he *has* to go into the world, in unconditional love, in order to meet God; for 'God is love' and 'he who does not love does not know God'.

And this profoundly affects the 'matter' of his prayer. Let us listen again to George Macleod:

> What debilitates our prayer life ... is our presupposition that the pressures of life are on one side while God is on some other side: interested and concerned but on some other side. With this supposition, when evening comes with an ending to our pressures, we are apt to go eagerly to God—disconcertingly to

find a vacuum. We seek to fill the vacuum with 'spiritual thoughts'. The more we try the more desperate does the situation become: till in effect we say that we are not really the praying type. Thus we begin to lean perilously to one side of the knife-edge.

There are, of course, evenings when our prayer-life is refreshing: but, analysed, they turn out to be the times when the pressures have been so weighty that you have simply had to go with them to God. But this precisely is the recovery of the knife-edge. The religious moment flowers from the practical. Of the prayer life, too, we can come to say, 'Hereby know we that we are passed from death unto life, *because we love the brethren*'.[1]

I believe that our teaching on prayer must begin not from 'finding God in the gaps' (let alone from looking for him only 'on the borders' 'where human powers give out',[2] which is the point at which popular men 'turn to prayer'), but from taking the world, history, the diary, seriously as the locus of incarnation. The 'matter' of prayer is supplied by the world—that is why too rarefied an atmosphere may be *harder* to pray in as it is to breathe in. The Christian life, the life of 'the man for others', must, as Bonhoeffer insisted,[3] be a 'worldly' life. Yet it must be a life of 'holy worldliness',[4] of 'sacred secularity'.[5]

And this means seeing the diary *in depth*, preparing in the telephone to meet our *God*. And that cannot be done by skating across the surface of life; it can only be done by 'waiting upon the Lord', but waiting upon the Lord like Nehemiah with a trowel in one hand and a sword in the other. And so, as it were, with the engagement pad and the

---

[1] *Op. cit.*, p. 160.
[2] Bonhoeffer, *Letters and Papers from Prison*, p. 124.
[3] *Op. cit.*, p. 166.
[4] A. R. Vidler, *Essays in Liberality* (1957), Ch. V.
[5] M. A. C. Warren, *CMS Newsletter*, No. 252, September 1962.

newspaper spread before the Lord, George Macleod describes
the function of morning prayer:

> We resolutely count out the paper money of our plotted day
> till we have assessed its value in the coinage of the eternal. In
> the light of the Incarnation nothing is secular. But unless we
> handle each paper token of the seeming secular and hold it
> till we see its true value in the light of the glorified humanity
> then, by ten of the morning, we are down one precipice of the
> knife-edge and are in a like judgement with the pietist who has
> gone down the other side.[1]

Prayer is openness to the ground of our being; and in it
'the readiness is all'. This means, as we shall see to be the
case with ethics, that it is impossible to compile a prayer
manual comparable with the old guides to 'the spiritual
life'.[2] If prayer is what you do when you turn aside into
'the hidden garden', then you can to some extent plot its
paths and cultivate its borders. 'Meditation' can be con-
ducted like a laboratory experiment, with its conditions laid
down beforehand and its methods pre-selected. But if we
really take seriously the fact that the Lord must meet us
first on the Emmaus road before he can turn in to 'abide
with us', then there are no ready-made rules. The words,

> If on our daily course our mind
> Be set to hallow *all* we find,

provide no reliable guide to the religious life. But they may
be the only condition of prayer.

Moreover, if prayer does not start from 'the spaces', then
to fix the spaces as if they were primary and all else would
follow may be the path to disillusionment. Indeed, I believe

---

[1] *Op. cit.*, p. 161.
[2] A phrase incidentally which is not Biblical. If the New Testament
used it it would describe the whole of the new life in the Spirit—not 'the
religious quarter'.

this is why countless people give up praying. They set aside the spaces religiously, and they become emptier and emptier. I am not suggesting in the least that the spaces are not necessary, but I believe they will not be creative until they are *seen* to be necessary, made imperative by the overspill of a prayer-laden life. In fact, if I had the courage, I would start the other end in teaching the discipline of prayer—not from *chronos*, time set by the clock, but from *kairos*, waiting for the moment that drives us to our knees. I am only too conscious that this is dangerous doctrine and that the casualties may be many—though would they be more numerous than those of our present methods? Such an approach requires greater self-discipline, not less. But before it is dismissed as the laxest of all rules of life, I would urge a comparison. There are those who keep fit, and feel they can only keep fit, by a rigid 'constitutional' each day; there are others who reckon to keep in trim by using their common sense, taking exercise as and when they really feel they need it. There are students who can only keep up to the mark by setting themselves a strict quota of hours of study each day; there are others who trust themselves to work responsibly and play responsibly. There are those who know they can control their spending only by keeping detailed accounts; there are others who are content to rely on their bank statements and a day-to-day judgement of what they can rightly afford.

Our Victorian grandparents believed in the constitutional, in the time-table, and above all in keeping accounts, almost as religiously as some priests now prescribe a rule of life. But one wonders whether there may not for some types be as much liberation in their abandonment as in their observance, and in the end no less discipline. Of course, we may easily grow fat, lax and spendthrift, and in our spiritual

account who can be confident how he stands? Nevertheless,
let a man but sense the binding power of the unconditional
over his life at some point, however non-religious, let him
but know with any depth or passion that 'persons matter',
let him but feel any constraint of the love of Christ, then
the chances are that that man's life will have an inner
discipline—and a compulsion to prayer—more effective
than that of any artificial rules. Rules, guiding lines, checks
and balances, there must be, but for 'man come of age',[1]
however unregenerate, they are bound to be different—and
more dangerous. But in the freedom with which Christ has
set us free we must accept and even welcome that risk.
There is little hope, in any case, in simply beating the old
drum. We shall not impose a religious discipline except on
the religious—that is (to use the analogy with St Paul's
controversy with the Judaizers), on 'man under the law'.
Man today is no longer content to be 'under tutors'. Yet
he must discover—and discover for himself—that he will
be free only 'within the law of Christ', as the bondservant
of Love. The words of St Augustine, 'Love God, and do
what you like', were never safe. But they constitute the
heart of Christian prayer—as they do of Christian conduct.

   And to this we must now turn, if we are to explore the
full consequences of Christianity 'in an entire absence of
religion'.

---

[1] The phrase is perhaps unfortunate in so far as it suggests an
emotional or moral maturity, which Bonhoeffer never implied (least
of all in his captors!). 'When we speak of God in a non-religious way',
he said, 'we must not gloss over the ungodliness of the world, but
expose it in a new light. Now that it has come of age, the world is more
godless, and perhaps it is for that very reason nearer to God than ever
before' (*op. cit.*, p. 167). For the educated minority this 'coming of age'
does indeed imply an intellectual maturity, but in most merely a
psychological stage of development in which religion and its attempt
to keep man in strings is dismissed as childish. But it is none the less
real for that.

6

'THE NEW MORALITY'

The Revolution in Ethics

PRAYER and ethics are simply the inside and outside of
the same thing. Indeed, they could both be defined, from
the Christian point of view, as meeting the unconditional
in the conditioned in unconditional personal relationship.
And it is impossible to reassess one's doctrine of God, of
how one understands the transcendent, without bringing
one's view of morality into the same melting-pot. Indeed,
the two are inseparable. For assertions about God are in
the last analysis assertions about Love—about the ultimate
ground and meaning of personal relationships. As John
Wren-Lewis puts it, interpreting the teaching of the Prophets
and the New Testament,

> Moral assertions about human interrelationship are not
> derived 'at second hand' from the fact that the Being called
> 'God' just happens to be interested in justice—they are
> directly and integrally bound up with assertions about God's
> Being *in itself*.[1]

But there is no need to prove that a revolution is required
in morals. It has long since broken out; and it is no 'reluctant
revolution'. The wind of change here is a gale. Our only
task is to relate it correctly to the previous revolution we
have described and to try to discern what should be the
Christian attitude to it.

There are plenty of voices within the Church greeting it

[1] *They Became Anglicans*, pp. 170 f.

with vociferous dismay. The religious sanctions are losing their strength, the moral landmarks are disappearing beneath the flood, the nation is in danger. This is the end-term of the apostasy from Christianity: the fathers rejected the doctrine, the children have abandoned the morals. Indeed, we could use almost unaltered the words quoted earlier from Bonhoeffer about the process of secularization: 'Catholic and Protestant . . . are agreed that it is in this development that the great defection from God, from Christ, is to be discerned, *and the more they bring in and make use of God and Christ in opposition to this trend, the more the trend itself considers itself to be anti-Christian*'.[1] And therein, of course, lies the danger. Christianity is identified *tout court* with the old, traditional morality. That would not matter if this morality were Christian. But in fact it is the equivalent in the ethical field of the supranaturalist way of thinking. And though this undoubtedly served the Church in its day, and still seems perfectly adequate—and indeed vitally necessary—to the religious, it would be calamitous if we allowed Christianity to be dismissed with it. And precisely that is what we are encouraging.

To this way of thinking right and wrong *are* derived 'at second hand' from God. They are the commandments which God gives, the laws which he lays down. According to the classic mythological statement of this position, they are delivered to Moses on the mountain top, graven on tablets. They come down direct from heaven, and are eternally valid for human conduct. But in morals as in metaphysics, the transition from the God 'up there' to the God 'out there' has long since been made, and these 'absolute standards' are normally now presented for our obedience stripped of their mythological garb. They may as a result

[1] *Op. cit.*, p. 146. Italics mine.

be thought of more in terms of 'natural law' than of 'positive law', but they are still written into the universe, they are still 'given', objectively and immutably. Certain things are always 'wrong' and 'nothing can make them right', and certain things are always 'sins', whether or not they are judged by differing human societies to be 'crimes'. The supreme example of this way of thinking is, of course, the corpus of Roman Catholic moral theology, and it is magnificent in its monolithic consistency. But it is a way of thinking that pervades, even if in more muddled form, the whole of the Church's ethical teaching, Catholic and Protestant, official and unofficial.

A conspicuous example of this is the traditional thinking on one of the most hotly debated of moral issues, that of marriage and divorce. There are, of course, widely divergent views within the Church on this question, even within what might be called the supranaturalist camp. There is, for instance, a deep division on the interpretation of the 'indissolubility' of marriage. There are those who say that 'indissoluble' means 'ought not to be dissolved', ought *never* to be dissolved. There are others who take it to mean 'cannot be dissolved': a physical or metaphysical union is created by wedlock which cannot be abrogated any more than two persons can cease to be brother and sister. This latter view is in fact an interesting example of a way of thinking that has characterized the whole supranaturalistic view of the world and which Dr Wren-Lewis has analysed in his essay 'The Decline of Magic in Art and Politics'.[1] This is the supposition that the network of empirical relationships is but a veil for a world of occult realities which lie behind the outward order of things and constitute the truth about man or society or nature, however much the

[1] *The Critical Quarterly*, Spring 1960, pp. 7-23.

empirical facts may appear to dispute it. 'The divine right of kings' is an example, or the medieval doctrine of 'signatures', or of 'degree'—the mystical hierarchy based on 'primogeniture and due of birth'. Behind the empirical relationships there are invisible realities, essences, structures, whose validity, grounded in the eternal order of things, is independent of anything that can be inferred or questioned from the phenomena. To this same category belongs the notion that the essence of marriage is a metaphysical or quasi-physical reality, constituted by the sacrament, which endures quite independently of the actual quality of the personal relationship or any indication that it may for all practical purposes be non-existent. The reality cannot be affected by any empirical facts or undone by any legal fiction. According to this version of the supranaturalist view, divorce is quite literally, and not merely morally, impossible. It is not a question of 'Those whom God hath joined together *let* no man put asunder': no man could if he tried. For marriage is not merely indissoluble: it is indelible.

There are those who are ready enough to borrow arguments—and apparently invincible arguments—from this way of thinking to uphold 'the sanctity of marriage', but it is questionable how many today really believe this form of the doctrine that 'marriages are made in heaven'. It is certain at any rate that their chances of commending it are small indeed to a world in full retreat on every front—scientific, political, artistic and religious—from such an occult view of life. Moreover, and more important, it is far from obvious that it has any basis in the teaching of Jesus or the New Testament. There is nothing specifically Christian about it, any more than there is about the mythological world-view. It is simply the metaphysic of a pre-scientific

age. To tie Christianity to it is simply to ask for the one to be discredited with the other.

But there is another version of the supranaturalist ethic of marriage which is much more widespread, especially among Protestants. This bases marriage, like all else in life, upon the absolute command or law of God, or upon the teaching of Christ interpreted in the same legalistic manner. According to this view, God has laid down 'laws which never shall be broken'. Divorce is always and absolutely wrong. If any accommodation is made to it, it is 'for the hardness of men's hearts'. But in any case they must be made to realize from what they are falling short. For the 'absolute moral standard' is written and engraven for all to see. The supranaturalist ethic has behind it the sanction of Sinai and 'the clear teaching of our Lord'. There can be no doubt about Christian standards in this or any other matter. In any change they are unchangeable: the only question is whether men live up to them. The task of the Church is to recall men to them, and to the religion on which they are based.

This position has a far wider popular appeal. It is indeed what men expect the Church to stand for—and for anyone, especially a bishop, to appear to contradict it is regarded as profoundly shocking. But equally obviously it is a position that men honour much more in the breach than the observance. The sanctions of Sinai have lost their terrors, and people no longer accept the authority of Jesus even as a great moral teacher. Robbed of its supernatural supports, men find it difficult to take seriously a code of living that confessedly depended on them. 'Why shouldn't I?' or 'What's wrong with it?' are questions which in our genera-tion press for an answer. And supranaturalist reasons—that God or Christ has pronounced it 'a sin'—have force, and even meaning, for none but a diminishing religious remnant.

But is it not perhaps for such a remnant that the Christian ethic is intended? There is, indeed, no sanction in the Gospels for believing that the gate is anything but narrow, 'and few there be that find it'.[1] But equally there is no suggestion in the Gospels that the Christian ethic is for 'the religious' only. It is for all men: it is based upon the nature of man, and for the foundation of his teaching on marriage Jesus specifically went behind Moses and the Law to creation.[2] It is for all men universally: it is not for *homo religiosus*.

The Teaching of Jesus

A much more fundamental criticism of this supranatural-istic ethic than that it now restricts its relevance to those who can accept its foundation is that it seriously distorts the teaching of Jesus. 'The clear teaching of our Lord' is taken to mean that Jesus laid down certain precepts which were universally binding. Certain things were always right, other things were always wrong—for all men everywhere.

But this is to treat the Sermon on the Mount as the new Law, and, even if Matthew may have interpreted Jesus that way, there would hardly be a New Testament scholar today who would not say that it was a misinterpretation. The moral precepts of Jesus are not intended to be understood legalis-tically, as prescribing what all Christians must do, whatever the circumstances, and pronouncing certain courses of action universally right and others universally wrong. They are not legislation laying down what love always demands of every one: they are illustrations of what love may at any

[1] Matt. 7.14.   [2] Mark 10.2-9.

moment require of anyone.[1] They are, as it were, parables
of the Kingdom in its moral claims—flashlight pictures of
the uncompromising demand which the Kingdom must
make upon any who would respond to it. The word to the
rich young man, 'Go and sell all that you have',[2] is not a
universal principle of the ethical life, but as it were a translation into the imperative of the parable of the rich merchant,
who went and did just this for the pearl of great price.[3]
This transition to the imperative—'Go and do likewise'[4]—
is not legislation, but a way of saying, as Nathan said to
David at the close of the classic parable of the Old Testament, 'You are the man'.[5] It is a reminder that the parables
are precisely not interesting stories of general application,
but the call of the Kingdom to a specific group or individual
at a particular moment.

This insistence on the parabolic character of the ethical
sayings of Jesus should deliver us from the danger of taking
them either as literal injunctions for any situation or as
universal principles for every situation. The Sermon on the
Mount does not say in advance, 'This is what in any given
circumstances you must do', but, 'This is the kind of thing
which at any moment, if you are open to the absolute,
unconditional will of God, the Kingdom (or love) can
demand of you'. It is relevant not because it provides us
with an infallible guide to the moral life, but because as
Martin Dibelius put it, 'we are able to be transformed by it'.

Jesus' teaching on marriage, as on everything else, is not
a new law prescribing that divorce is always and in every
case the greater of two evils (whereas Moses said there were
some cases in which it was not). It is saying that love,

---

[1] See especially C. H. Dodd, *Gospel and Law* (1951).
[2] Mark 10.21. [3] Matt. 13.46.
[4] Luke 10.37. [5] II Sam. 12.7.

utterly unconditional love, admits of no accommodation; you cannot define in advance situations in which it can be satisfied with less than complete and unreserved self-giving. It may mean selling all one possesses,[1] putting one's whole livelihood in the collection,[2] giving up one's clothes or lending one's money entirely without question,[3] cutting off one's right hand or pulling out one's eye.[4] Yet equally clearly not every situation will demand this, and Jesus' sayings make no attempt to adjudicate on conflicting claims[5] or to take into account the needs of third persons such as every real-life situation raises (e.g., who is going to maintain the widow after she has pledged her total means of support or the children of the man who has given everything to a beggar). Of course, love must consider these—and equally unreservedly. Jesus never resolves these choices for us: he is content with the knowledge that if we have the heart of the matter in us, if our eye is single, then love will find the way, its own particular way in every individual situation.

What the supranaturalist ethic does is to subordinate the actual individual relationship to some universal, whether metaphysical or moral, external to it. The decision is not reached, the judgement is not made, on the empirical realities of the particular concrete relationship between the persons concerned. Man is made for the sabbath, and not the sabbath for man. Be the individual circumstances what they will, the moral law is the same—for all men and for all times. It is imposed on the relationship from without, from above: the function of casuistry is to 'apply' it *to* the case in question.

Such an ethic is 'heteronomous', in the sense that it derives its norm from 'out there'; and this is, of course,

---

[1] Mark 10.21.   [2] Mark 12.44.   [3] Matt. 5.40, 42.
[4] Matt. 5.29 f.   [5] Luke 12.14.

its strength. It stands for 'absolute', 'objective' moral values
and presents a dyke against the floods of relativism and
subjectivism. And yet this heteronomy is also its profound
weakness. Except to the man who believes in 'the God out
there' it has no compelling sanction or self-authenticating
foundation. It cannot answer the question '*Why* is this
wrong?' in terms of the intrinsic realities of the situation
itself.

The revolt in the field of ethics from supranaturalism to
naturalism, from heteronomy to autonomy, has been with
us so long that we need not spend much time on it. It began
with the magnificent grandeur of Kant's autonomous ideal,
perhaps the greatest and most objective of all ethical systems.
But this was really only secularized deism—and not completely secularized at that; for though Kant dispensed with
the hypothesis of God to account for the source of the moral
law, he brought him back, as a very crude *deus ex machina*,
to ensure the eventual coincidence of virtue and happiness.
Kant's moral idealism was living on religious capital. As
this ran out or was rejected, it came to be replaced by every
kind of ethical relativism—utilitarianism, evolutionary
naturalism, existentialism. These systems, so different in
themselves, have this in common: they have taken their
stand, quite correctly, against any subordination of the
concrete needs of the individual situation to an alien
universal norm. But in the process any objective or unconditional standard has disappeared in a morass of relativism
and subjectivism. Tillich sums up the situation in words
that refer to culture in general but apply just as much to its
ethical aspect:

> Autonomy is able to live as long as it can draw from the
> religious tradition of the past, from the remnants of a lost
> theonomy. But more and more it loses this spiritual founda-

tion. It becomes emptier, more formalistic, or more factual and is driven towards scepticism and cynicism, towards the loss of meaning and purpose. The history of autonomous cultures is the history of a continuous waste of spiritual substance. At the end of this process autonomy turns back to the lost theonomy with impotent longing, or it looks forward to a new theonomy.[1]

What does Tillich mean by this word 'theonomy'? It corresponds with his concern to push 'beyond supra-naturalism and naturalism' to a third position, in which the transcendent is nothing external or 'out there' but is encountered in, with and under the *Thou* of all finite relation-ships as their ultimate depth and ground and meaning. In ethics this means accepting as the basis of moral judgements the actual concrete relationship in all its particularity, refusing to subordinate it to any universal norm or to treat it merely as a case, but yet, in the depth of that unique relationship, meeting and responding to the claims of the sacred, the holy and the absolutely unconditional. For the Christian it means recognizing as the ultimate ground of our being which is thus encountered, and as the basis of every relationship and every decision, the unconditional love of Jesus Christ, 'the man for others'. This is what it means for the Christian to 'have the mind of Christ',[2] to let his actions be governed, as Jesus enjoined, simply and solely by the love with which 'I have loved you',[3] or, in St Paul's words, to 'let your bearing towards one another arise out of your life in Christ Jesus'.[4] Life in Christ Jesus, in the new being, in the Spirit, means having no absolutes but his love, being totally uncommitted in every other respect but totally committed in this. And this utter openness in love to the 'other' for his own sake is equally the only

---

[1] *The Protestant Era*, p. 53.   [2] I Cor. 2.16.
[3] John 13.34.   [4] Phil. 2.5 (NEB).

absolute for the non-Christian, as the parable of the Sheep and the Goats shows. He may not recognize Christ in the 'other' but in so far as he has responded to the claim of the unconditional in love he has responded to him—for he is the 'depth' of love. The Christian ethic is not relevant merely for the Christian, still less merely for the religious. The claim of the Christ may come to others, as indeed it often comes to the Christian, incognito: but since it is the claim of home, of the personal ground of our very being, it does not come as anything foreign. It is neither heteronomous nor autonomous but theonomous.

Love alone, because, as it were, it has a built-in moral compass, enabling it to 'home' intuitively upon the deepest need of the other, can allow itself to be directed completely by the situation. It alone can afford to be utterly open to the situation, or rather to the person in the situation, uniquely and for his own sake, without losing its direction or unconditionality. It is able to embrace an ethic of radical responsiveness, meeting every situation on its own merits, with no prescriptive laws. In Tillich's words, 'Love alone can transform itself according to the concrete demands of every individual and social situation without losing its eternity and dignity and unconditional validity'.[1] For this reason it is the only ethic which offers a point of constancy in a world of flux and yet remains absolutely free for, and free over, the changing situation. It is prepared to see every moment as a fresh creation from God's hand demanding its own and perhaps wholly unprecedented response. And that is why Tillich goes on, 'Ethics in a changing world must be understood as the ethics of the *kairos*'—of the God-given moment, mediating the meeting with the eternal in the temporal. 'Love, realizing itself from *kairos* to *kairos*,

[1] *The Protestant Era*, p. 173.

creates an ethics which is beyond the alternative of absolute
and relative ethics'[1]—or what he elsewhere calls supranaturalism and naturalism.

Nothing Prescribed—Except Love

This position, foreshadowed thirty years ago in Emil
Brunner's great book, *The Divine Imperative*,[2] is given its
most consistent statement I know in an article by Professor
Joseph Fletcher in the *Harvard Divinity Bulletin*,[3] entitled
'The New Look in Christian Ethics'. 'Christian ethics', he
says, 'is not a scheme of codified conduct. It is a purposive
effort to relate love to a world of relativities through a
casuistry obedient to love.'[4] It is a radical 'ethic of the
situation', with nothing prescribed—except love.

It is, like classical casuistry, case-focussed and concrete,
concerned to bring Christian imperatives into practical operation. But unlike classical casuistry, this neo-casuistry repudiates
the attempt to anticipate or prescribe real-life decisions in
their existential particularity. There is after all no discredit to
the old-fashioned casuists, nor to the Talmudists, in the old
saying that they continually made rules for the breaking of
rules. They were turning and twisting in their own trap to
serve love as well as law, but unfortunately the only result is a
never ending tangle of legalism in any ethics which attempts
to correct code law with loving kindness. The reverse of these
roles is vitally necessary. It is love which is the constitutive
principle—and law, at most, is only the regulative one, if it
is even that.[5]

The classic illustration of this insistence in the teaching
of Jesus, that the sabbath is made for man and not man for
the sabbath, that compassion for *persons* overrides all law,
is his shocking approbation of David's action in placing

---

[1] *Op. cit.*, p. 173.   [2] 1932, Eng. tr. 1937.
[3] October 1959, pp. 7-18.   [4] *Op. cit.*, p. 10.   [5] *Op. cit.*, p. 17.

human need (even his own) above all regulations however sacrosanct:

Have you not read what David did, when he was hungry, and those who were with him: how he entered the house of God and ate the bread of the Presence, which it was not lawful for him to eat nor for those who were with him, but only for the priests?[1]

It is, of course, a highly dangerous ethic and the representatives of supranaturalistic legalism will, like the Pharisees,[2] always fear it. Yet I believe it is the only ethic for 'man come of age' To resist it in the name of religious sanctions will not stop it: it will only ensure that the form it takes will be anti-Christian. For as Fletcher says,

Torah law in this era is suffering a second eclipse, even more radical than when Jesus and St Paul first attacked it—because the cultural-context, the milieu controls, are more appropriate today to such an eclipse than in the apostolic and patristic period.[3]

The fact that the old land-marks are disappearing is not something simply to be deplored. If we have the courage, it is something to be welcomed—as a challenge to Christian ethics to shake itself loose from the supports of supranaturalistic legalism on which it has been content to rest too much. And this is bound to be disturbing. To quote Fletcher again,

This contemporary shape of Christian ethics was accurately described and labelled as 'existential' or 'situational' by Pope Pius XII in an allocution on April 18, 1952.[4] He denounced it, of course, pointing out that such a non-prescriptive ethic might be used to justify a Catholic leaving the Roman Church if it seemed to bring him closer to God, or to defend the

[1] Matt. 12.3 f. See the whole context Matt. 12.1-14.
[2] Matt. 12.14.   [3] *Op. cit.*, p. 15.
[4] *Acta Apostolicae Sedis*, (1952), xliv, pp. 413-19.

practice of birth control just because personality could be enhanced thereby! Four years later, February 2, 1956, the Supreme Sacred Congregation of the Holy Office called it 'the New Morality' and banned it from all academies and seminaries, trying to counteract its influence among Catholic moralists.[1]

But of course Protestant and Anglican reaction is equally suspicious when it becomes clear what judgements it may lead to or what rules and sanctions it appears to jeopardize.

For nothing can of itself always be labelled as 'wrong'. One cannot, for instance, start from the position 'sex relations before marriage' or 'divorce' are wrong or sinful in themselves. They may be in 99 cases or even 100 cases out of 100, but they are not intrinsically so, for the only intrinsic evil is lack of love. Continence and indissolubility may be the guiding norms of love's response; they may, and should, be hedged about by the laws and conventions of society, for these are the dykes of love in a wayward and loveless world. But, morally speaking, they must be defended, as Fletcher puts it, 'situationally, not prescriptively'—in other words, in terms of the fact that persons matter, and the deepest welfare of these particular persons in this particular situation matters, more than anything else in the world. Love's casuistry must cut deeper and must be more searching, more demanding, than anything required by the law, precisely because it goes to the heart of the individual personal situation. But we are bound in the end to say with Professor Fletcher: 'If the emotional and spiritual welfare of both parents and children in a *particular* family can be served best by a divorce, wrong and cheapjack as divorce commonly is, then love requires it'.[2]

This will once again be greeted as licence to laxity and

[1] *Op. cit.*, p. 16.   [2] *Op. cit.*, p. 15.

to the broadest possible living. But love's gate is strict and narrow and its requirements infinitely deeper and more penetrating. To the young man asking in his relations with a girl, 'Why shouldn't I?', it is relatively easy to say 'Because it's wrong' or 'Because it's a sin'—and then to condemn him when he, or his whole generation, takes no notice. It makes much greater demands to ask, and to answer, the question 'Do you love her?' or '*How much* do you love her?', and then to help him to accept *for himself* the decision that, if he doesn't, or doesn't very deeply, then his action is immoral, or, if he does, then he will respect her far too much to use her or take liberties with her. Chastity is the expression of charity—of caring, enough. And this is the criterion for every form of behaviour, inside marriage or out of it, in sexual ethics or in any other field. For *nothing else* makes a thing right or wrong.[1]

This 'new morality' is, of course, none other than the old morality, just as the new commandment is the old, yet ever fresh, commandment of love.[2] It is what St Augustine dared to say with his *dilige et quod vis fac*,[3] which, as Fletcher rightly insists,[4] should be translated not 'love and do what you please', but 'love and *then* what you will, do'. *What* 'love's casuistry' requires makes, of course, the most searching demands both upon the depth and integrity of one's concern for the other—whether it is really the utterly unselfregarding *agape* of Christ—and upon the calculation of what is truly the most loving thing in this situation for every person involved. Such an ethic cannot but rely, in deep humility, upon guiding rules, upon the cumulative experience of one's own and other people's obedience. It is

[1] See the essay on 'The Virtue of Chastity' in J. Macmurray, *Reason and Emotion* (1935), and H. A. Williams, 'Theology and Self-Awareness', in *Soundings*, pp. 81 f.
[2] I John 2.7 f.   [3] *Ep. Joan.* vii. 5.   [4] *Op. cit.*, p. 10.

this bank of experience which gives us our working rules of 'right' and 'wrong', and without them we could not but flounder. And it is these, constantly re-examined, which, in order to protect personality, have to be built into our codes of law, paradoxically, 'without respect of persons'. But love is the end of law[1] precisely because it *does* respect persons—the unique, individual person—unconditionally. 'The absoluteness of love is its power to go into the concrete situation, to discover what is demanded by the predicament of the concrete to which it turns.'[2] Whatever the pointers of the law to the demands of love, there can for the Christian be no 'packaged' moral judgements—for persons are more important even than 'standards'.

Seeking to retain his integrity in these judgements will inevitably bring the Christian into conflict with the guardians of the established morality, whether ecclesiastical or secular. He may often find himself more in sympathy with those whose standards are different from his own and yet whose rebellion deep down is motivated by the same protest on behalf of the priority of persons and personal relationships over any heteronomy, even of the supranatural. For many of these may be feeling their way through to a new theonomy to which the Christian must say 'yes', even if the *theos* is not 'the God and Father of our Lord Jesus Christ'. D. H. Lawrence, for instance, comes very near to what we have been saying when in speaking of that which is at the heart and depth of a person, he writes:

> And then—when you find your own manhood—your womanhood . . . —then you know it is not your own, to do as you like with. You don't have it of your own will. It comes from—from the middle—from the God. Beyond me, at the middle, is the God.[3]

[1] Rom. 13.10.   [2] Tillich, *Systematic Theology*, vol. i, p. 169
[3] *The Plumed Serpent* (1926), Phoenix edition, p. 70.

'God is the "beyond" in the midst of our life': Bonhoeffer's words[1] are almost identical. 'The God,' no doubt, is very different;[2] but at least there is a way through here to the transcendent in a world without religion. And on that 'way' the Christian must be found if he is to say anything to those who walk along it. In morals, as in everything else, 'the secret of our exit' from the morasses of relativism is not, I believe, a 'recall to religion', a reassertion of the sanctions of the supranatural. It is to take our place alongside those who are deep in the search for meaning *etsi deus non daretur*, even if God is not 'there'. It is to join those on the Emmaus road who have no religion left,[3] and there, in, with and under the meeting of man with man and the breaking of our common bread, to encounter the unconditional as the Christ of our lives.

[1] *Op. cit.*, p. 124.
[2] For a balanced Christian assessment of Lawrence's understanding of God, cf. M. Jarrett-Kerr, *D. H. Lawrence and Human Existence* (2nd ed., 1961), pp. 129-57.
[3] Luke 24.21.

RECASTING THE MOULD

The Images Which Can Be Discarded

'WHAT we call Christianity has always been a pattern—perhaps a true pattern—of religion,' wrote Bonhoeffer on April 30, 1944.[1]

> Our whole nineteen-hundred-year-old Christian preaching and theology rests upon the 'religious premise' of man. . . . But if one day it becomes apparent that this *a priori* 'premise' simply does not exist, but was an historical and temporary form of self-expression, i.e., if we reach a stage of being radically without religion—and I think this is the case already, else how is it, for instance, that this war, unlike any of those before it, is not calling forth any 'religious' reaction?—what does that mean for Christianity'?
>
> It means that the linchpin is removed from the whole structure of our Christianity to date.[2]

Bonhoeffer here draws a distinction between the Gospel and 'Christianity' as a 'pattern of religion'. This is a distinction which it is extremely difficult for us to grasp, since, as he says, the two have been identified in our minds for 1900 years. We are just beginning to get used to the idea that 'Christendom' may be a historically conditioned phenomenon—appearing on the European scene with Constantine and gradually disappearing over the last five hundred years. But can we—should we—accustom ourselves to think of 'Christianity' itself, as an organized religion, in the same sort of terms? I am not sure yet whether we can fully understand the question, let alone give the answer.

[1] *Op. cit.*, p. 122.   [2] *Ibid.*

What I want to attempt in this chapter is a more limited undertaking, namely, to consider some of the implications of what I have been saying for our present 'pattern of religion'. We shall not abolish it, even if we wanted to. But in a situation where this pattern is for most people indistinguishable, even in theory, from the Gospel, it is important to try to see what consequences follow and what do not. It will doubtless seem to some that I have by implication abandoned the Christian faith and practice altogether. On the contrary, I believe that *unless* we are prepared for the kind of revolution of which I have spoken it *will come* to be abandoned. And that will be because it is moulded, in the form we know it, by a cast of thought that belongs to a past age—the cast of thought which, with their different emphases, Bultmann describes as 'mythological', Tillich as 'supranaturalist', and Bonhoeffer as 'religious'.

It may be easier for us to recognize this if we look first not at our own situation but at one which, though not strictly parallel (since it involved the preaching of a new gospel altogether), has sufficient similarities to be instructive.

'In the law', says St Paul of the Jews, 'you see the very shape (*morphosis*) of knowledge and truth.'[1] That was their glory—and their liability. They had it all—the very 'oracles of God',[2] 'the splendour of the divine presence'[3]—and yet none of it possessed any validity for them except within a certain fixed 'pattern of religion': the Law was the mould that shaped everything into acceptability. St Paul, indeed, will not hear a word against the Law as such: it is 'holy and just and good'.[4] And yet the time came when it was to prove the stumbling-block to knowing the very God whose truth it existed to shape.

[1] Rom. 2.20 (NEB).　　[2] Rom. 3.2.　　[3] Rom. 9.4.　　[4] Rom. 7.12.

Bonhoeffer, as we have seen, regarded 'the religious premise' today as comparable with this presupposition of the Law which stood between the Jew and the Gospel. Once again, we must insist, there is nothing wrong as such with the God of the religious premise, with 'the One above' to whom the religious person instinctively 'turns'—provided he be truly the God and Father of our Lord Jesus Christ. Such a religious pattern holds for him 'the very shape of knowledge and truth'—and woe betide the one who would wantonly shatter it. It has been—and still is for millions— the precondition of the Presence. And yet, as John D. Godsey observes in his book on Bonhoeffer, 'The continuance of a "religious" interpretation of the gospel in a "nonreligious" world may be at once a misunderstanding of the gospel itself and a default of the Church's responsibility vis-à-vis the world. Bonhoeffer has posed this question in a way that cannot be ignored.'[1]

What looks like being required of us, reluctant as we may be for the effort involved, is a radically new mould, or *meta-morphosis*, of Christian belief and practice. Such a recasting will, I am convinced, leave the fundamental truth of the Gospel unaffected. But it means that we have to be prepared for *everything* to go into the melting—even our most cherished religious categories and moral absolutes. And the first thing we must be ready to let go is our image of God himself.

The need for this is again perhaps best brought out by looking at the other great debate in which Paul was engaged —not, this time, with the Jews to whom the Gospel was a stumbling-block, but with the Greeks to whom it was folly.[2] The classic description of this debate is to be found in his

---

[1] *The Theology of Dietrich Bonhoeffer*, pp. 17 f.
[2] I Cor. 1.23.

encounter with the intelligentsia of his day on the Areopagus at Athens.[1]

Here, so far from the accepted mould of religious truth proving an insuperable barrier, there was apparently no point of contact at all. His gospel seemed utterly incomprehensible. 'What is this new teaching?' they asked in ridicule and contempt. The same question, though with a different slant, had been asked by the crowds of Jesus when he began his public ministry: 'What is this new teaching?'[2] And so it has always been. Paul was dismissed as a setter forth of strange gods, Socrates was condemned as an 'atheist'. Every new religious truth comes as the destroyer of some other god, as an attack upon that which men hold most sacred.

It is easy for us to persuade ourselves that this is a process which lies now in the past, that Christianity has supplanted the idols of heathenism and that we now know the one true God. But in fact the debate staged on the Areopagus is a debate that is never closed. It has constantly to be reopened, as one idol is knocked down, only to be replaced by another. For the Christian gospel is in perpetual conflict with the images of God set up in the minds of men, even of Christian men, as they seek in each generation to encompass his meaning. These images fulfil an essential purpose, to focus the unknowable, to enclose the inexhaustible, so that ordinary men and women can get their minds round God and have something on which to fix their imagination and prayers. But as soon as they become a substitute for God, as soon as they *become* God, *so that what is not embodied in the image is excluded or denied*, then we have a new idolatry and once more the word of judgement has to fall. In the pagan world it was—and still is—a matter in the main of metal images. For us it is a question much more of mental

[1] Acts 17.16-34.   [2] Mark 1.27.

images—as one after another serves its purpose and has to go.

I tried to trace earlier the way in which successive images of God, 'up there' and 'out there'—seemingly in their time indispensable as a focus for any conception of deity—can, gradually or even quite suddenly, become meaningless or worse. I cited[1]—simply as an illustration of one alternative—Tillich's description of God as the 'depth' of life. I have since used that quotation in a diocesan publication. It evoked two replies—one of profound gratitude from someone for whom it had lit up entirely afresh the meaning of God; the other from a deeply sincere orthodox Churchman for whom it seemed blasphemous heresy.

I have a great deal of sympathy with those who react in this latter way: it is as much my God as theirs that seems to be in jeopardy. But I have a great deal of sympathy also with those who call themselves atheists. For the God they are tilting against, the God they honestly feel they cannot believe in, is so often an image of God instead of God, a way of conceiving him which has become an idol. Paul had the perception to see that behind the idols of the Athenians there was an unknown, an unacknowledged God, whom dimly they sensed and felt after. And to help men through to the conviction about ultimate Reality that alone finally matters we may have to discard every image of God—whether of the 'one above', the one 'out there', or any other. And this conviction, according to the Christian gospel, is that

> there is nothing in death or life, . . . in the world as it is or the world as it shall be, in the forces of the universe, in heights or depths—nothing in all creation that can separate us from the love of God in Christ Jesus our Lord.[2]

[1] P. 22 above.   [2] Rom. 8.38 f., NEB.

That I believe with all my being, and that is what at heart it means to be a Christian. As for the rest, as for the images of God, whether metal or mental, I am prepared to be an agnostic with the agnostic, even an atheist with the atheists. Such is the release I find in the story of St Paul's great encounter with the men of Athens.

But having said that, I should like to define and guard my position further on two flanks, the one against non-Christian naturalism, the other against 'orthodox' supra-naturalism.

Christianity and Naturalism

Julian Huxley, in his persuasive book of that title, argues that the end of supernaturalism means 'religion *without revelation*'. The discrediting of 'the god hypothesis' throws him back upon a religion of Evolutionary Humanism. 'My faith', he says in his closing sentence, 'is in the possibilities of man.'[1]

But it is precisely the thesis of this book that this is not the only alternative. I am convinced, as I have said, that we should follow Huxley, who is here at one with Bonhoeffer, in discarding the supranaturalist framework. But whereas Huxley does it in the interest of religion without revelation, Bonhoeffer does it in the interest of Christianity without religion—not, of course, that Bonhoeffer desires to abolish religion, in the way that Huxley wants to dispense with revelation: he simply wishes to free Christianity from any necessary dependence upon 'the religious premise'.

The essential difference can perhaps best be brought out by reverting to the distinction between the apparently similar affirmations that 'God is love' and that 'love is God'.

[1] *Op. cit.*, p. 239.

For the humanist, to believe in a 'religion of love' is to affirm
the conviction that love *ought to be* the last word about life,
and to dedicate oneself to seeing that it everywhere prevails.
Thus Professor R. B. Braithwaite maintains that to assert
that God is love (*agape*) is to declare one's 'intention to
follow an *agapeistic* way of life'.[1] Belief is the avowal of a
policy, the declaration that love is the supremely valuable
quality. And such belief, of course, requires no revelation.

But the Christian affirmation is not simply that love
ought to be the last word about life, but that, despite all
appearances, it *is*. It is the conviction, again, that 'there is
nothing . . . in the world as it is or the world as it shall
be . . . that can separate us from the love of God in Christ
Jesus our Lord'. And that takes an almost impossible amount
of believing. It is frankly incredible *unless* the love revealed
in Jesus is indeed the nature of ultimate reality, unless he is
a window through the surface of things into *God*. Christianity
stands or falls by revelation, by Christ as the disclosure of
the final truth not merely about human nature (that we
might accept relatively easily) but about all nature and all
reality. The Christian's faith cannot rest in the capacities of
man. Indeed, it strikes him as astonishing that someone of
Huxley's honesty and intelligence should be able to reissue
his book in 1957 without a single reference to the possibility,
not to say probability, that there might not, within his
frame of reference, be any prospects for humanity at all.
No, the Christian's faith is in Christ as the revelation, the
laying bare, of the very heart and being of ultimate reality.
And that is why, in the categories of traditional theology,
it was so necessary to insist that he was *homousios*, of one
substance, with the Father. For unless the *ousia*, the being,
of things deep down *is* Love, of the quality disclosed in the

[1] *An Empiricist's View of the Nature of Religious Belief* (1955), p. 18.

life, death and resurrection of Jesus Christ, then the Christian could have little confidence in affirming the ultimate personal character of reality. And this—not his religiosity, nor his belief in the existence of a Person in heaven—is what finally distinguishes him from the humanist and the atheist.

This distinction may be clarified by comparison with another great non-Christian of our day, Albert Camus, whose entirely 'non-religious' description of the human situation in *The Fall* is incidentally a good deal nearer to the Christian estimate of man than Huxley's. While Huxley writes as the religious man, for whom the God of supra-naturalist Christianity is a stumbling-block, for Camus the entire schema appears folly. His novel, *The Outsider*, ends with the prison chaplain trying in vain to make any sense of God to the homicide in his cell. After a final outburst against everything the priest stands for, the condemned man concludes, in the closing sentences of the book:

> It was as if that great rush of anger had washed me clean, emptied me of hope, and, gazing up at the dark sky spangled with its signs and stars . . ., I laid my heart open to the benign indifference of the universe. To feel it so like myself, indeed so brotherly, made me realize that I'd been happy, and that I was happy still. For all to be accomplished, for me to feel less lonely, all that remained was to hope that on the day of my execution there should be a huge crowd of spectators and that they should greet me with howls of execration.[1]

Such is the universe which for 'the outsider' is home. The contrast in Bonhoeffer's letters from prison could hardly be greater. And yet they both speak in a situation *etsi deus non daretur*, of man for whom the consolations of religion, the *deus ex machina*, the god-hypothesis, are dead beyond recall. The Christian is the man who *in that situation*

[1] *The Collected Fiction of Albert Camus* (1960), p. 68.

still knows that 'home' is Christ and that to be 'in him' is to lay himself open, not to the benign indifference, but to the divine *agape*, of the universe, to feel it so like himself, so brotherly. For that in the last analysis is what it means to be convinced of the personality, of the Christ-likeness, of God.

Christianity and Supranaturalism

But what does this mean, on the other flank, for the representatives of traditional supranaturalism? They may find it difficult to believe that it must not result in a theology of mere immanence, not to say of pantheism. And it is perhaps necessary to rebut rather carefully the suspicion of pantheism, which must doubtless cling to any reconstruction that questions the existence of God as a *separate* Being. For traditionally, the immanentist or pantheistic world-view has been countered in deism and theism with the assertion that the world owes its origin to *a* Creator, an almighty Artificer, who at a moment of time (or 'with' time) 'made' it 'out of nothing'.

This is clearly a highly mythological and anthropomorphic picture. But it is entirely possible to demythologize it without lapsing into pantheism. The essential difference between the Biblical and any immanentist world-view lies in the fact that it grounds all reality ultimately in personal freedom—in Love. For pantheism, the relation of every aspect of reality to its ground is in the last analysis a deterministic one, allowing no real room for freedom or for moral evil. It finds its natural expression in the mechanical or organic categories of emanation or evolution rather than in the personal categories of creation. But the Biblical affirmation is that built into the very structure of our relationship to the ground of our being is an indestructible element of personal freedom. We are not like rays to the sun or leaves to the tree: we are united to the source, sustainer and goal of our life in a relationship whose only analogy is that of *I* to *Thou*—except that the freedom in which we are held is one of utter dependence. We are rooted and grounded wholly in Love. And the doctrine of creation *ex nihilo* is that there is nothing in us or in 'all creation' which has ultimately to be attributed to some other ground or found some other explanation.

It is this freedom built into the structure of our being which gives us (within the relationship of dependence) the independence, the 'distance', as it were, to be ourselves. What traditional deism and theism have done is to 'objecti-vize' this distance into the pictorial image of a God 'out there'. But the projection of God *from* the world as a super-Individual is no more necessary an expression of trans-cendence than is mileage upwards from the earth's surface. They are both but objectifications in the language of myth—in terms of 'another' world—of the transcendental, the unconditional in all our experience. The test of any restate-ment is not whether this projection is preserved but whether these elements are safeguarded. And that I believe I have tried to do.

All true awareness of God is an experience at one and the same time of ultimacy *and* intimacy, of the *mysterium tremendum et fascinans*. It may be psychologically inevitable that the recognition of 'the infinite qualitative difference' between the Creator and the creature, between the holy God and sinful man, should find its symbolic expression in the cry, 'Depart from me'[1]—that is, in the setting of *space* in between. And it may be impossible to *imagine* the personal ground of all our being except as an almighty

[1] Luke 5.8.

Individual, endowed with a centre of consciousness and will like ourselves and yet wholly 'other'. As symbols these images have their powerful and their proper place. They become idols only when the images are regarded as indispensable for the apprehending of the reality; they become dangerous only when they cease to mediate the reality and indeed become barriers to it. To demythologize—as Bultmann would readily concede—is not to suppose that we can dispense with all myth or symbol. It is to cut our dependence upon one particular mythology—of what Tillich calls the 'superworld of divine objects'—which is in peril of becoming a source of incredulity rather than an aid to faith. Any alternative language—e.g. of depth—is bound to be equally symbolic. But it may speak more 'profoundly' to the soul of modern man.

Moreover, there are whole areas of response where the myth still occasions little difficulty. In prophecy and prayer, in liturgy and worship, the traditional imagery retains its numinous power.

Thus saith the high and lofty one that inhabiteth eternity . . .
Our Father, which art in heaven . . .
Therefore with angels and archangels . . .

Every generation can make such language its own, whatever the mould of its belief, whatever its projection of God. Liturgy, indeed, is the main medium of that transposition of which I spoke earlier,[1] whereby we can readily accept and use a notation that on the face of it belongs to an entirely alien thought-world. In fact, as Canon Hugh Montefiore observes in another connection,[2] our impasse is primarily an intellectual one.

[1] P. 13 above.
[2] 'Towards a Christology for Today', in *Soundings*, pp. 161 f.

It does not immediately or directly affect Christian faith or Christian worship or the conduct of the Christian life. God is still at work. The old formulas continue to be used: they serve in worship, they comprise pictorial imagery useful for meditation, and they mark the continuity of our faith and devotion with that of our Christian ancestors. They preserve what may be meaningless to one generation but meaningful to the next. Our search is *fides quaerens intellectum*: and so long as the search can and does continue, the insufficiency of our theology need not affect Christian faith or conduct or worship.

But the proviso is all important. Without the constant discipline of theological thought, asking what we really mean by the symbols, purging out the dead myths, and being utterly honest before God with ourselves and the world, the Church can quickly become obscurantist and its faith and conduct and worship increasingly formal and hollow. That is why the cast of our theology, the mould of our belief, is in the long run so important. It will condition everything. But I have not attempted here to traverse the full range of Christian doctrine. I have simply been engaged upon a probing operation—trying to see at certain fundamental points of faith and practice what it may mean, as I put it earlier, to question one whole set of presuppositions and feel towards another in its place.

Consequences for the Church

Still less has it been my intention to map a new programme. Nevertheless, it is only fair that I should say something of the practical consequences of what I have propounded for the life and strategy of the Church. For they are bound to be in the minds both of the proponents and of the opponents of 'organized religion'.

What a fearful phrase this is when one stops to think

about it, and how calamitous that Christians should have
come to find themselves committed to its defence. That the
Church has a concern with religion—as with every other
aspect of human life—no one would doubt. That it must
be organized—and efficiently organized—is equally clear.
But that Christianity should be equated in the public mind,
inside as well as outside the Church, with 'organized
religion' merely shows how far we have departed from the
New Testament. For the last thing the Church exists to be
is an organization for the religious. Its charter is to be the
servant of the world.

One might think this too obvious to need saying, but,
alas, it does not require much research to come upon the
kind of article from which Dr Vidler starts his chapter on
'Religion and the National Life' in the collection of essays
called *Soundings*[1] to which I have already referred. 'The
church is primarily a religious organization', says its writer,
'and the Christian gospel caters for the religious needs of
man. It is the job of the church to preach, to pray, to sing
hymns and to encourage and develop the pious feelings of
its members. . . . Religion is not concerned with the whole
of life, but with a part of life.'[2]

Admittedly this is a rich specimen, and my immediate
reaction was to suppose that these sentences must surely
have been taken out of context. But I was to find that the
half had not been told. 'What can be done to make the
church more religious?' the author went on. 'Certainly
something must be done. . . . We must . . . increase our
emphasis upon the church as a *religious* organization with a
limited purpose.'[3]

[1] P. 241.
[2] David Nicholls, 'Your God is Too Big!', *Prism*, July 1961, p. 22.
[3] *Op. cit.*, pp. 22 f. Italics his.

Whatever else the Church must be organized for, it cannot be primarily for this. But it is much harder to give a positive answer to another string of tantalizing questions posed by Bonhoeffer:

> What is the significance of a Church (church, parish, preaching, Christian life) in a religionless world? . . . In what way are we in a religionless and secular sense Christians, in what way are we the *Ekklesia*, 'those who are called forth', not conceiving of ourselves religiously as specially favoured, but as wholly belonging to the world?[1]

He left indications that he thought the answers would be pretty radical. 'By the time you are grown up', he wrote to a godson, 'the form of the Church will have changed beyond recognition.'[2] And in his 'Outline for a Book' the final chapter was to begin:

> The Church is her true self only when she exists for humanity. As a fresh start she should give away all her endowments to the poor and needy. The clergy should live solely on the freewill offerings of their congregations, or possibly engage in some secular calling. She must take her part in the social life of the world, not lording it over men, but helping and serving them. She must tell men, whatever their calling, what it means to live in Christ, to exist for others.[3]

On this Dr Vidler comments:

> It is consistent with accepting Bonhoeffer as a prophet for our time to acknowledge that, like other prophets, he saw things too much in black and white and also that he foreshortened the realization of what he expected, as when he told his godchild that, *by the time he was grown up*, the form of the Church would have changed beyond recognition.[4]

[1] *Op. cit.*, p. 123. Earlier, in his *Ethics* (1955), p. 21, he had used these striking words: 'The Church is nothing but a section of humanity in which Christ has really taken form. The Church is the man in Christ, incarnate, sentenced and awakened to new life.'
[2] *Letters and Papers from Prison*, p. 140.   [3] *Op. cit.*, p. 180.
[4] *Op. cit.*, p. 253.

Nevertheless, I believe that Bonhoeffer was right in his assessment of the *direction* in which the Church must move. And on this direction I should like to say a few words in closing.

Nothing that has been said so far should be taken to imply that an indispensable task of the Church is not what the Collect[1] calls the 'increase' of 'true religion'. This, of course, is the concern that underlay the article we dragged out for pillory. Unless the Church has the 'secret discipline' of which Bonhoeffer spoke as the presupposition of all his 'worldly Christianity',[2] unless the Christian's 'life is hid with Christ in God',[3] then any distinction between being *in* the world but not *of* it disappears, and at once he is down one side of the 'knife-edge'. There must be what Jacques Ellul has called a distinctively Christian 'style of life',[4] and if this is not nourished all is lost. Yet even this is not best described in religious terms, as it is not confined to the sphere of religion. As Ellul, the layman, puts it, 'the whole of life is concerned' in it. 'It includes the way we think about present political questions as well as our way of practising hospitality.'[5] And Professor Gregor Smith in trying to expound Bonhoeffer's meaning says:

> It is a kind of humorous, humble, self-effacing secrecy of devotion and hope, which finds no counterpart in the visible world, nothing in symbol or gesture by which it may be fully reflected and expressed. . . . Nevertheless it is there, and the simplicities of the gospel, the call to be humble, and un-ostentatious in prayer, never using naked power, but always

[1] For the seventh Sunday after Trinity.
[2] *Op. cit.*, pp. 123, 126: cf. earlier, *The Cost of Discipleship* (1948) and *Life Together*.
[3] Col. 3.3.
[4] *The Presence of the Kingdom* (1951), pp. 145-50. For an expansion of this concept, cf. F. O. Ayres, *The Ministry of the Laity* (1962).
[5] *Op. cit.*, p. 148.

service, and sacrifice, are both its sustenance and its preservative.[1]

And this, so far from requiring the stepping up of the Church as a religious organization, points rather in the direction of the *dépouillement* or stripping down which Bonhoeffer believed it must undergo.

This could be put in another way by saying that the Church must become genuinely and increasingly *lay*—providing we understand that much misused word aright. This does not mean its becoming a lay movement, in the sense of abolishing its sacramental ministers (even Bonhoeffer's most radical vision did not include that). For to define the laity in opposition to the priesthood is itself one of the by-products of clericalism. Rather, the laity is the *laos* or people of God *in the world*. And what Bonhoeffer meant by authentic Christian worldliness is echoed quite independently by the Roman Catholic, Fr Yves Congar, in his designation of a layman[2] as one for whom the things of this world are 'really interesting *in themselves*', for whom 'their truth is not as it were swallowed up and destroyed by a higher reference'—for instance, by how far they can be turned to the service of the Church or used as occasions for evangelism.[3] And this is a temper of mind, a genuine 'laicity' (to use Congar's term) which need not, indeed cannot, be confined to those who are not ordained. It must be the temper of the whole Church, if it is really to be the representative of 'the man for others'. So again Ronald Gregor Smith writes:

What the world would really see gladly is an honest and complete recognition, without any ulterior motives, by those

[1] *Op. cit.*, pp. 104 f.
[2] *Lay People in the Church* (1959), pp. 17-21.
   Cf. D. Jenkins, *Beyond Religion*, p. 22.

who claim to carry forward the message of Christianity, of the existence of the world with all its own principles of movement, hopes and possibilities.[1]

The Church, he goes on,

needs to recognize the hidden unconditional ground even in the most autonomous of human pursuits, it needs to welcome those pursuits not for the hope that they may be violently 'baptized' into Christ, but for their own sake. . . . If the unity of truth and being in Christ is more than a piece of sentimentalizing, then this identifying of oneself fully with the things and the people of the world is in fact an absolutely necessary step in the same direction taken by the incarnate Lord, who took upon himself the form of a servant in absolute seriousness and not merely as a docetic whimsy.[2]

What this means in detailed terms for the structure or strategy of the Church I do not propose to pursue here. It will vary so much in every local situation. The specific for Bonhoeffer's war-weary Germany or for the United States today[3] or for the emergent nations of Africa is obviously very different. I am not greatly excited by the current signs of the survival of religiousness in Russia or of its revival in America. It may even confirm, as Daniel Jenkins has suggested,[4]

Oswald Spengler's remarkable prophecy of a generation ago, in *The Decline of the West*, when he spoke of the appearance of 'a second religiousness' which is, according to him, the sign

---

[1] *Op. cit.*, p. 69.

[2] *Op. cit.*, pp. 69 f. Cf. N. Pittenger, 'Secular Study and Christian Faith', *Theology*, vol. lxv (February 1962), pp. 45-51.

[3] Cf. the notable series of analyses of the American 'religious establishment': Will Herberg, *Protestant-Catholic-Jew* (1955); Martin E. Marty, *The New Shape of American Religion* (1959); Gibson Winter, *The Suburban Captivity of the Churches* (1961); and (I think most excitingly) Peter L. Berger, *The Noise of Solemn Assemblies* (1961). The last works out the percipient but dangerous proposition: 'Involvement with organized religion is a Christian vocation' (p. 174).

[4] *Op. cit.*, pp. 100 f.

that a culture is drawing to the end of the cycle of its life.[1] The present revival shows enough of the conservatism of outlook, the nostalgia for the past, and the stylization which are characteristic of 'second religiousness' to suggest that the possibility that it will evaporate in this way is a real one.

I would not presume to make such a judgement, and I do not want in the least to dispute its sincerity. I merely raise the question whether, amid all the drives of modern secular society, whether collectivized or cybernated,[2] the main function of the Church is to make or to keep men religious. I doubt whether it helps to answer the question of how to commend Christianity in a post-religious age. In fact, it probably hinders it. 'We have been all too ready', says Ronald Gregor Smith, 'especially since the great break-through of the Renaissance, to fight a kind of battle against the world on behalf of God'.[3] I would see much more hope for the Church if it was organized not to defend the interests of religion against the inroads of the state (legitimate and necessary as this may be) but to equip Christians, by the quality and power of its community life, to enter with their 'secret discipline' into all the exhilarating, and dangerous, secular strivings of our day, there to follow and to find the workings of God.

With regard to my own Church of England, I find myself in wide measure of agreement with both the hopes and the fears expressed by Dr Vidler.[4] Anything that helps to keep its frontiers open to the world as the Church of the nation should be strengthened and reformed: anything that turns it in upon itself as a religious organization or episcopalian

[1] *Op. cit.*, (1918-22) Eng. tr. (1926-8), vol. ii, pp. 310-15.
[2] Cf. the fascinating and frightening report by D. N. Michael, *Cybernation: The Silent Conquest* (1962) on the social prospects of automation. It is available free, on request, from The Center for the Study of Democratic Institutions, Box 4068, Santa Barbara, California.
[3] *Op. cit.*, pp. 98 f.   [4] *Op. cit.*, pp. 255-63.

sect I suspect and deplore. For the true radical is not the
man who wants to root out the tares from the wheat so as
to make the Church perfect: it is only too easy on these
lines to reform the Church into a walled garden. The true
radical is the man who continually subjects the Church to
the judgement of the Kingdom, to the claims of God in the
increasingly non-religious world which the Church exists to
serve.

I have not attempted in this book to propound a new
model of the Church or of anything else. My aim has been
much more modest. I have tried simply to be honest, and
to be open to certain 'obstinate questionings' which speak
to me of the need for what I called earlier a reluctant
revolution. In it and through it, I am convinced, the funda-
mentals will remain, but only as we are prepared to sit
loose to fundamentalisms of every kind. In the oft-quoted
words with which Professor Herbert Butterfield ends his
Christianity and History,[1]

> There are times when we can never meet the future with
> sufficient elasticity of mind, especially if we are locked in the
> contemporary systems of thought. We can do worse than
> remember a principle which both gives us a firm Rock and
> leaves us the maximum elasticity for our minds: the principle:
> Hold to Christ, and for the rest be totally uncommitted.

This basic commitment to Christ may have been in the
past—and may be for most of us still—buttressed and
fortified by many lesser commitments—to a particular
projection of God, a particular 'myth' of the Incarnation,
a particular code of morals, a particular pattern of religion.
Without the buttresses it may look as if all would collapse.
Nevertheless, we must beware of clinging to the buttresses
instead of to Christ. And still more must we beware of

[1] 1949, p. 146.

insisting on the buttresses as the way to Christ. For to growing numbers in our generation they are barriers rather than supports. Let the Editor of *Prism*[1] speak for them:

> Whether it is true, as Bonhoeffer evidently thought, that the *'homo non religiosus'* is in bulk a new phenomenon, I do not know. What certainly is true is that there are many men who find traditional religion and spirituality completely meaningless, and that you will find them among those who are completely committed to Christ as well as among those that are not. . . . We have reached a moment in history when these things are at last being said openly and when they are said there is an almost audible gasp of relief from those whose consciences have been wrongly burdened by the religious tradition.

It is also true that when they have been said we are still only at the beginning of our task. But the beginning is to try to be honest—and to go on from there. And that is what in a very preliminary, exploratory way this little book has attempted to do.

[1] September 1962, pp. 2 f.

INDEX

HONEST TO GOD IN NORTH AMERICA

DOUGLAS JOHN HALL

Professor Emeritus of Christian Theology,
McGill University

HONEST to God burst in upon the scene of our rather smug, though faltering, ecclesiastical discourse on this continent just as I began my professional life as a teaching theologian. Personally, I found the book stimulating. All the same, I'd have been glad to leave it on the shelf so far as my classroom was concerned—though of course I did not, could not. I did not feel then that the churches in North America were ready to tackle such an intensive rethinking of the basics. Most of them, including the candidates for ministry whom I had been employed to teach, had not thought "the basics" even once, in any concentrated way, let alone being in a position to *re*think them!

The background out of which Bishop Robinson spoke was quite different from that of most of his readers: he was a seasoned, professional biblical scholar and theologian who, having lived intimately with the tradition, began to find it problematic as he faced, concretely, the task of episcopal oversight and the communication of the faith in a postreligious society. In this capacity he felt obliged to become, as he said, the advocate of a "reluctant revolution"[1]—*reluctant* because, as a serious scholar of the doctrinal traditions of Christendom, he had a respectful awareness of their profundity. He was not an iconoclast, self-righteously bent on clearing the household of faith of all its doctrinal bric-a-brac. If he was driven to raise "revolutionary" questions about what he had

---

[1] *Honest to God* (London: SCM Press; Philadelphia: Westminster Press, 1963), 11–28.

been "handed over" (*tradere*), it was not for want of reverence but because he understood its treasures well enough to realize that, without removing them from the "earthen vessels" of the out-moded metaphysics and anachronistic dogmas in which they were encased, they would be lost to the contemporary mind-set, and, in all probability, to the church itself.

Not only did Robinson speak out of a scholar's awareness of the great tradition, he was also (as *Honest to God* itself demonstrates) knowledgeable concerning twentieth-century developments in Christian theology. As Theodore O. Wedel, Canon Theologian of the Cathedral of St. John the Divine in New York City, remarked in a review, "The Bishop of Woolwich is not committing a crime in revealing to a wider public what has been going on for a gener-ation and longer in the world of advanced theological learning."[2] Those who found Robinson's musings shocking evidently had lit-tle awareness of the "Teutonic mentors" on whose work he drew (Tillich, Bultmann, and Bonhoeffer), nor of the others on whom he might have drawn, including Karl Barth.[3] As Martin E. Marty remarked in a *Christian Century* review, "Track the Teutonic lions to their lairs and you will hear more ominous growlings any day of the week than this genteel book emits!"[4]

Unfortunately, nothing remotely approaching Robinson's knowledge of either contemporary theology or the classical doc-trines of Christendom could be counted on in the churches—at least the churches in North America, where theological inquiry

[2] David L. Edwards, ed., *The Honest to God Debate* (London: SCM Press; and Philadelphia: Westminster Press, 1963), 181.

[3] John C. Bennett, among others, felt that the omission of Barth from Robinson's purview was unfortunate: "Barth is the great theolo-gian of God's freedom, and this book might have been better if Barth had been allowed to influence it." See "A Most Welcome Event," *Christianity and Crisis* 23, no. 19 (November 11, 1963): 202.

[4] Martin E. Marty, "The Bishop and the Debate," *Christian Cen-tury* (June 24, 1964): 830.

and the pursuit of understanding, as de Tocqueville had judiciously observed long before,[5] was rarely associated with popular religion.[6] What *could* be assumed in this context in 1963, moreover, far from constituting an aid to any measured reception of Robinson's critique, represented a deterrent to the same; for, among the most vocal elements in the churches, one was conscious of a vague dissatisfaction with the status quo, a bourgeois restlessness with "religion" as a whole, a spiritual disquiet articulate in a few but merely brooding and disgruntled in the majority. The euphoria of the postwar period was over; the churches' building spree of the 1950s had (mercifully!) spent itself; and the great countercultural revolt of the '60s and early '70s was just about to erupt. The time was ripe, it would seem, for a Christian battle cry. And that, I think, was how Robinson's book functioned within the churches of the Protestant mainstream, the original intentions of its author notwithstanding.

The result was that a book that might have brought illumination and sober reflection to a province of the church badly in need of these brought agitation and turbulence more often than it did clarity. For those who shared something of Robinson's deep indoctrination in the tradition, *Honest to God* could and often did highlight the very questions they had been silently nursing. (I remember well the enthusiasm of an urbane Dutch

[5] In America, "'the majority draws a formidable circle around thought. Within its limits, one is free; but woe to him who dares to break out of it.' Religion, [de Tocqueville] saw, was a major element in the formation of this circle. He believed there was no country in the world where the Christian religion retained a greater influence over the souls of men than in America." Martin E. Marty, *Righteous Empire: The Protestant Experience in America* (New York: Harper Torchbooks, 1970), 90.

[6] "A great distance separates the thinking of sophisticated theologians from the actual teaching done in the churches. We have always known this was true, but the sale of this book dramatizes the fact." Bennett, "A Most Welcome Event," 201.

theologian, the late Ellen Flessemann–van Leer, who was visiting Canada at this time, and who, when I asked for her reaction to the new book, beamed, "I wish I had written it!")[7] But these were the exceptions. Many clergy and students of theology, possessing that "dangerous thing," "a little learning," fastened on the more outspoken statements of the book and made them rallying points for their own largely inchoate feelings or causes. If their inclinations were conservative, they could damn the bishop; if liberal, they could claim, as they thought, his episcopal blessing![8]

This was only the beginning of an entire epoch in North American Christianity that was punctuated by little books which, often independently of their authors' aims, functioned to fill the vacuum of purpose and direction in the churches and to fuel the fires of polarization. After *Honest to God* and *The Honest to God Debate*[9] came Harvey Cox's *The Secular City*,[10] J. C. Hoekendijk's *The Church Inside Out*,[11] Albert van dan Heuvel's *The Humiliation of*

---

[7] Paul Lehmann registered a similar appreciation for Robinson's book: "He has brought the concerns and wrestlings of theological scholarship during the past quarter-century into confrontation with the world's puzzlement and indifference to Christian faith and life. . . . What Bishop Robinson has written deserves the most serious and searching attention." *Christianity and Crisis* 23, no. 19 (November 11, 1963): 199.

[8] Lehmann was particularly scornful of such critics: "Only the most intransigent orthodoxy of piety and of theology will find in this attempt to be 'honest to God' a sign of the continuing havoc wrought upon the Church by a critical theology. The obsolescence of such an orthodoxy is patent." Ibid., 198–99.

[9] D. L. Edwards, ed. (London: SCM Press; Philadelphia: Westminster Press, 1963).

[10] Harvey Cox, *The Secular City* (New York: Macmillan Co., 1965).

[11] J. C. Hoekendijk, *The Church Inside Out*, ed. L. A. Hoedemaker and Pieter Tijmes, trans. Isaac C. Rottenberg (Philadelphia: Westminster Press, 1966 [Dutch version: *De kerk binnenste buiten,* Amsterdam: W. ten Have, 1964]).

the Church,[12] Gabriel Vahanian's *Wait without Idols*,[13] Paul van Buren's *The Secular Meaning of the Gospel*,[14] and others. Then, by the late '60s, we were into the "death of God" theologies, attended by a whole spate of "theologies of" (secularity, celebration, hope, liberation), accompanied or followed by black theology; feminist/ womanist theologies; ecological, peace, and justice theologies; theologies of sexuality, and so on—all of them investigations inspired by concern for some forgotten, submerged, or deliberately marginalized aspect of the tradition, usually embraced in the name of a particular identity or issue.

All of them were, in one way or another, to one degree or another, *quite necessary*, I should judge, to the further investigation and propagation of the Christian faith. Nevertheless, the real service such works could perform for the Christian movement as it tried to make its way into the future beyond the impasse of modernity depended for its efficacy on a greater awareness of (and, as I shall argue in the conclusion, a greater commitment to) the whole tradition than could be assumed in the North American churches. Where these "new" theologies inspired the depth of rethinking/reimagining that their authors themselves, most of them, could claim, or where, in the process of upholding their particular points of view, they also undertook a teaching ministry for those who could not make such a claim, the thinking and decision making they inspired really could be appreciated as a renewal of faith.[15] But where their impassioned messages fell on the rocky

---

[12] Albert van dan Heuvel, *The Humiliation of the Church* (London: SCM Press, 1967).

[13] Gabriel Vahanian, *Wait without Idols* (New York: George Braziller, 1964).

[14] Paul van Buren, *The Secular Meaning of the Gospel* (New York: Macmillan Co.; London: SCM Press, 1963).

[15] As was the case with process theology and the theology of hope, as well as of some feminist theologies.

ground of biblical and doctrinal ignorance or naïveté, as it more frequently did, they brought agitation without illumination, enthusiasm without wisdom.

Perhaps that is, after all, quite predictable and usual. History does not wait for a public that is mature before it introduces its various revolutions! All the same, experience shows, I think, that a public that has lost touch with its own foundational assumptions is not only often at the mercy of "enthusiasm" (*Schwärmerei*), but does grave injustice to its own more *responsible* reformers and prophets by hearing their critique without the benefit of comprehending the "system" being criticized. Such a public takes the *results* of its reformers' struggles (rather, *some* of the results) without sharing the painful process of deriving them.

Where Christianity is concerned, this is an especially important observation. For the hope that Christians entertain, though it is forever in need of restatement (*semper reformanda*) depends on a lively remembrance of what has been handed over. That is why all great reformations of the Christian movement, including the Reformation of the sixteenth century, involve both a forward and a backward look. Think of Luther's dependence on Augustine! Hope will be recognizably "Christian" only when it grows out of a fresh wrestling with the collective historical memory of the community of discipleship as it encounters new barriers to its credibility. A church that neglects its ongoing dialogue with its past (Scripture, tradition, and history) is hardly prepared to benefit from the critical promptings of its own best seers. For even more than democratic society depends on a continuous dialogue with the ideological roots of democracy, a faith that locates its very center in a historical Event must continuously rehearse the faith it *professes* if it is to be moved by its teachers and sages to *confess* its faith in the here and now.

This, I believe—this "professional" awareness of the faith on the part of the whole *laos*—is what was missing, and on the whole is missing still, throughout the epoch (1960 to the present) that saw the influence of the many provocative works of which Robinson's *Honest to God* was the first. The impact of Robinson's book in the North American churches could have been much more helpful and lasting, as well as more consistent with the aims of its author, had the churches been better informed about the traditions the book called into question and about the whole course of late nineteenth and early twentieth century theology. Since they were not, the profundity of Bishop Robinson's critique was missed, its nuances exchanged for slogans and one-sided summations, and its *quite constructive* suggestions for moving beyond the confrontation of "supernaturalism" and "naturalism" left largely untried. While there were certainly individual exceptions to that generalization, the assessment holds, I believe, for the churches generally. Predictably enough, people aligned themselves either with the traditionalists Robinson *seems* to dismiss or with the radicals he *seems* to praise. Few, it appears to me, understood that Robinson's real alternative is neither traditionalism *nor* radicality but—in true English, Anglican (and perhaps after all somewhat necessarily Christian!) fashion—a via media.

The surest test of the appropriateness of that judgment is reading *Honest to God* forty years later, after the heat of its brief half-life as a media event, after the equally brief lives of its various successors, and in the face of the problems that it courageously tackled—problems that are still with us; problems that it might, under more auspicious contextual circumstances, have helped to resolve.

I shall elaborate on this interpretation by examining the four primary themes of *Honest to God*: (1) the author's own understanding of his program; (2) his critique of theology (i.e., conception of God); (3) his Christology/soteriology; (4) his conception of the Christian life. In each case, I want to show that the thrust of the book's message is a carefully nuanced, if insufficiently elaborated, position that is badly distorted when it feeds preexisting biases in its readers.

What Did Robinson Want to Accomplish?

A helpful device in interpreting the thought of another person, one that I learned from the late John Coleman Bennett, is to ask two questions: What is this person seeking to avoid? and What does he or she want to affirm or accomplish? Unlike some authors, Robinson was entirely open about what he feared and sought to avoid. He feared for the very survival of the faith: "*If Christianity is to survive,* let alone to recapture 'secular' man, there is no time to lose in detaching it from [supernaturalistic thought], . . . and thinking hard about what we should put in its place."[16] Toward the end of the book, he states this concern still more forcibly:

> It will doubtless seem to some that I have by implication abandoned the Christian faith and practice altogether. On the contrary, I believe that *unless* we are prepared for the kind of revolution of which I have spoken it *will come* to be abandoned. And that will be because it is moulded, in the form we know it, by a cast of thought that belongs to a past age—the cast of thought which, with their different emphases, Bultmann describes as 'mythological,' Tillich as 'supranaturalist,' and Bonhoeffer as 'religious'.[17]

These statements already imply what the bishop wished to *achieve or preserve,* but he could also express his positive aim more boldly. While admitting a sincere fellow feeling with "the orthodox Churchmen" who were critical of his position ("it is as much my God as theirs that seems to be in jeopardy"), he confesses that he has become particularly conscious, on the other hand, of those who are kept from faith by false conceptions of Christian belief emanating from this same inflexible orthodoxy. Saint Paul on Mars Hill, he notes, "had the perception to see that behind the idols of the Athenians there was an unknown, an unacknowledged God, whom dimly they sensed and felt after." Similarly, Robinson wishes "to

---

[16] Robinson, *Honest to God*, 43 (my italics).
[17] Ibid., 123.

help men through to the conviction about ultimate Reality that alone finally matters." And he defines that "conviction" by quoting Paul's summation in Romans 8:38: "There is nothing in death or life, . . . in the world as it is or the world as it shall be, in the forces of the universe, in heights or depths—nothing in all creation that can separate us from the love of God in Christ Jesus our Lord." "That," he concludes, "I believe with all my being, and that is what at heart it means to be a Christian. As for the rest, as for the images of God, whether metal or mental, I am prepared to be an agnostic with the agnostic, even an atheist with the atheists.[18] Such is the release I find in the story of St. Paul's great encounter with the men of Athens."[19]

In order to be perfectly clear about his method, Dr. Robinson goes on at once to explain this bold programmatic statement by identifying the (*nota bene*) *two* positions from which he intends to distinguish his own: "I should like to define and guard my position further on two flanks, the one against non-Christian naturalism, the other against 'orthodox' supranaturalism."[20]

Against naturalism, he defends *revelation* as the sine qua non of Christian faith. Julian Huxley argued that the end of supernaturalism had to mean "religion without revelation." With

[18] This is perhaps the kind of language that provoked in Alasdair MacIntyre the quite unhelpful and irresponsible charge that Robinson was "an atheist" ("God and the Theologians," in Edwards, *Honest to God Debate*, 215 ff.).

[19] Robinson, *Honest to God*, 126–27 (my italics).

[20] Ibid., 127 (my italics). Robert N. Bellah, then at Harvard, grasped this intention of the bishop in a way that many did not: "Robinson is saying plainly what the theologians he quotes have been saying involvedly. . . . Robinson and the major figures he quotes are not . . . liberals. They do not want to jettison great chunks of the tradition that they at the moment do not understand. They want to reinterpret what has become meaningless so that its message can communicate again. They are seeking for another way between liberalism and Barthianism." (However, a more informed commentator would have substituted "conservativism" for Bellah's "Barthianism.") See *Christianity and Crisis* 23, no. 19 (November 11, 1963): 200.

Bonhoeffer, to the contrary, Robinson's aim is to free Christianity from precisely *religion*, not from revelation. "Christianity stands or falls by revelation, by Christ as the disclosure of the final truth not merely about human nature . . . but about all nature and all reality."[21]

But contra supranaturalistic orthodoxy, Robinson insists that the doctrinal symbols of yesterday—such as that of "an almighty Individual, endowed with a centre of consciousness and will like ourselves yet wholly 'other'"—when they are presented as factual truths rather than images, become "idols" and "barriers" to belief. As images "they have their proper place"; yet without constantly undergoing theological interpretation and critique they function as "dead myths," inaccessible and unnecessarily offensive to thinking persons. "That is why the cast of our theology, the mould of our belief, is in the long run so important. It will condition everything."[22]

One cannot contemplate such an agenda today, especially in the light of the far more (in the popular sense) "radical" agendas that have been put forward since,[23] without wondering how so many could have heard it as a rank dismissal of tradition *or* as permission to proceed with a wholesale reworking of the faith along secular humanistic lines.[24] Clearly, Robinson was *trying* to sustain a position neither "liberal" nor "conservative"—one that could draw upon the *kerygmatic* foundations of the faith while simultaneously maintaining a strong *apologetic* concern

[21]   Ibid., 128.

[22]   Ibid., 133.

[23]   E.g., that of Bishop John Spong.

[24]   To those familiar with Tillich in particular, nothing in Robinson's book was either surprising or merely humanistic! Tillich was not then well known in England, as John Bennett remarked, but "To many of us in this country [the U.S.A.] *Honest to God* seems a delayed reaction to sermons preached by Paul Tillich in the Union Seminary chapel 20 years ago." Bennett, "A Most Welcome Event," 201.

for their communication. Just this, however, is the most difficult path to tread in our social and religious context; and, like many before and since, Bishop Robinson's rather carefully nuanced reflections were soon, with the excited help of the media, drawn into the familiar vortex of North America's almost pathological need to polarize.

Robinson's intention to steer between the Scylla of traditionalism and the Charybdis of secularist radicality is borne out in the main content areas of his small book.

Theology

What do Christians mean by "God"? Robinson devotes two chapters of *Honest to God* to that question. Using insights from three of his contemporaries (Tillich, Bultmann, and Bonhoeffer), though without making himself responsible for a full analysis of their work, Robinson declares that it is not only apologetically self-defeating but also theologically and biblically misleading to tie the Christian conception of deity to a "supranaturalistic" (Tillich), "mythological" (Bultmann), and "religious" (Bonhoeffer) worldview that is plainly obsolete. Christian faith does not consist in an *a priori* "theism" onto which the gospel is tacked. The old theism that began with proofs for the existence of God and presented reality "in terms of a three-storey universe with God up there, 'above' nature"[25] is simply an outmoded worldview. "Our concern is in no way to change the Christian doctrine of God but precisely *to see that it does not disappear with this outmoded view*."[26]

The key to disengaging God from the confining worldview with which Christian theology is intermingled is to appreciate divine transcendence differently from the "up there"/"out there"

[25] Robinson, *Honest to God*, 32.
[26] Ibid., 44 (my italics).

preconceptions of conventional religion. Tillich's use of episte-mological "depth" and of the phrase "ground of our being" to describe deity, as well as Bonhoeffer's sense of God as "the 'beyond' in the midst of life," suggest an approach to transcen-dence that does not rely on such preconceptions.

Yet Robinson is not about to concede that divine transcendence is just a product of human projection, à la Feuerbach. Some read-ers were surprised that the bishop found a certain Feuerbachian "ambiguity" in the thought of John Macmurray. Macmurray's view of the task of religion as "'the maintenance and extension of human community,'" prompts Robinson to ask: "if theology is translated into anthropology, why do we any longer need the category of God?"[27] Macmurray attributes transcendence to all human experi-ence and denies that it belongs to God uniquely. Robinson agrees that a quality of transcendence applies to all experience, but what we experience of *God's* transcendence is qualitatively different, for such experiences have about them the dimension of ultimacy (as in Tillich's "ultimate concern"). He writes: "There are depths of rev-elation, intimations of eternity, judgements of the holy and the sacred, awarenesses of the unconditional, the numinous and the ecstatic, which cannot be explained in purely naturalistic categories without being reduced to something else."[28] And he quotes Tillich: "To call God transcendent in this sense does not mean that one must establish a 'superworld' of divine objects. It does mean that, within itself, the finite world points beyond itself. In other words, it is self-transcendent."[29]

Robinson's intention of eliminating the supranaturalistic from Christian discourse about God does *not* entail, for him at least, the ("ambiguous") courting of the naturalistic antithesis that he finds

[27] Ibid., 51.   [28] Ibid., 55.

[29] Ibid., 55–56. The Tillich quotation is from Paul Tillich, *System-atic Theology,* vol. 2 (Chicago: University of Chicago Press, 1967), 7. (The reference in Robinson's text mistakenly cites p. 8).

in Macmurray (and also in some of John Wren-Lewis's state-ments). "God, the unconditional," he believes, "is to be found only in, with *and under* the conditioned relationships of this life: for he *is* their depth and ultimate significance."[30] But it is by no means enough to equate religion with human relationships and "commu-nity." "The necessity for the name 'God' lies in the fact that our being has depths which naturalism, whether evolutionary, mecha-nistic, dialectical or humanistic, cannot or will not recognize."[31]

In short, Robinson believes that the Christian confession of belief in God entails a critique of both the orthodox tendency to safeguard the deity against too great a proximity to humanity *and* the tendency of radical Christian humanism too easily to overcome the distance between God and the human.

Christology

A similar two-sided watchfulness informs Robinson's Christology/soteriology. A supranaturalistic conception of the Christ, popularized through "the 'magic' of Christmas," still dominates Christian piety, yet it renders the Christian witness falsely scan-dalous to contemporary thought, and it reduces the biblical testi-mony to the incarnation to absurdity. "The supranaturalist view of the Incarnation can never really rid itself of the idea of the prince who appears in the guise of a beggar. However genuinely destitute the beggar may be, he *is* a prince; and that in the end is what mat-ters."[32] Over against the tendency of popular preaching to announce, simply, "Jesus *was* God," in the New Testament "Jesus never claims to be God, personally."[33] The Scriptures will say that Jesus was God's "Word," or God's "Son," that God was "in Christ," and so on, but they do "not say that Jesus was God, simply like that."[34]

---

[30] Robinson, *Honest to God,* 60.
[31] Ibid., 54.
[32] Ibid., 67.
[33] Ibid., 70, 73.
[34] Ibid., 70.

Yet neither does the New Testament present Jesus merely as a man, another human being, or even (in a favorite liberal interpretation) a uniquely moral and God-inspired man. "There is a paradox running through all the Gospels that Jesus makes no claims for himself in his own right and at the same time makes the most tremendous claims about what God is doing through him and uniquely through him. . . . Jesus never claims to be God, personally: yet he always claims to bring God, completely."[35] But this seeming paradox is at the same time the (kenotic) clue to Jesus' supreme revelation of the love of God, as it is manifested on the cross. "For it is in this ultimate surrender of self, in love 'to the uttermost,' that Jesus is so completely united to the Ground of his being that he can say, 'I and the Father are one.'"[36]

Robinson's rejection of both popular orthodox and liberal views of Christ's *person* is followed through in the soteriology he sketches:

> In the case of the Atonement [most people] ask with some impatience how anything done two thousand years ago on the Cross *could* 'affect me now'. As a description of some metaphysical *opus operatum* the 'full, perfect and sufficient sacrifice, oblation, and satisfaction for the sins of the whole world' supposed to have been 'made' on Calvary requires, I believe, for most men today more demythologizing even than the Resurrection. At no point does the supranaturalist scheme appear less compelling.[37]

But this criticism of the dominant Latin (Anselmic or substitutionary) theory of atonement is matched by an equally serious criticism of the liberal "Moral Influence" theory: "At no point is the naturalistic view, even in its Liberal Christian form, shallower or more discredited than in its estimate of what is wrong with the world and of what is required to put it right."[38]

35 Ibid., 73.   36 Ibid., 74.
37 Ibid., 79.   38 Ibid.

Robinson's search for "a third alternative" to both positions certainly needs greater development than it is given in *Honest to God*; yet he indicates a clear direction when he quotes, at length, Paul Tillich's sermon "You Are Accepted"—which was one of Tillich's most successful attempts to render the Reformation's "justification by grace through faith" in contemporary language. Grace, Robinson insists, is certainly "beyond us," and therefore it cannot be "contained within any purely naturalistic categories." Yet neither is the "new reality" that is Christ's gift, transmitted to us through the divine Spirit, entirely discontinuous with our experience. It is "nearer to us than we are ourselves" (Tillich).

The Christian Life

The Christian community does not exist "to promote a new religion," writes Bishop Robinson in what may be one of the most evocative sentences of the book, "but simply to be the embodiment of this new being as love. And that means . . . 'participation in the powerlessness of God in the world' [Bonhoeffer]."[39] Obviously enough, it was not easy for the Bishop of Woolwich to absorb the full brunt of Dietrich Bonhoeffer's challenge to "religionless Christianity." He even allows himself at one point to quote Alec Vidler to the effect that Bonhoeffer, "like other prophets," sometimes "saw things too much in black and white."[40] And he shows a certain hesitancy on the whole question of Christian disestablishment that, had he lived

[39] Ibid., 82. Compare Jürgen Moltmann: "Jesus did not bring a new religion into the world but rather *new life*. What follows from this for the mission of Christians is the rebirth of life, arising from the proclamation of God's love for life." *A Passion for God's Reign*, ed. Miroslav Volf (Grand Rapids: Wm. B. Eerdmans Publishing Co., 1998), 61.

[40] Robinson, *Honest to God*, citing A. R. Vidler, "Religion and the National Church," *Soundings* (1962): 253.

another thirty of forty years, he might well have found rather precious.

All the same, he believed that Bonhoeffer "was right in his assessment of the *direction* in which the Church must move."[41] The church has to be concerned with religion. It must also be organized, "and efficiently organized." "But that Christianity should be equated in the public mind, inside as well as outside the Church, with 'organized religion' merely shows how far we have departed from the New Testament. For the last thing the Church exists to be is an organization for the religious. Its charter is to be the servant of the world."[42]

Of course, the church can only be such a worldly servant if the source of its life transcends the world. It is called to be "in" the world in compassion and solidarity, yet as a movement whose life is "hid with Christ in God." "There must be what Jacques Ellul has called a distinctively Christian 'style of life,' and if this is not nourished all is lost. Yet even this is not best described in religious terms."[43]

One senses in the concluding chapters of *Honest to God*, which concern the practical side of Robinson's "reluctant revolution," that the writer is groping for direction—as though he were at the edge of some Red Sea that he knows he must cross, yet senses how completely different from everything he has known life on the other side must be. His discussion of "The New Morality," with its agonizing over "marriage and divorce," is bound to seem dated in a context like ours, which has gone on to legal and sexual questions that quite eclipse the domestic perplexities of yesterday.

Yet in all his discussion of the Christian life, it is impossible to mistake Bishop Robinson's overarching desire to conserve what is best in the tradition and to make it speak to the here and now. He is prepared neither to jettison the past, whether in the

[41]   Ibid., 136.   [42]   Ibid., 134.
[43]   Ibid., 136.

realm of morality or in ecclesiological practice, nor to bow to the pressures of a one-dimensional secularity.

Conclusion

In one of the most perceptive contemporary reviews of *Honest to God*, Martin E. Marty speculated that, twenty years later, Bishop Robinson's best-seller would likely "deserve no more than a footnote" in any survey of theology in the twentieth century.[44] This prediction seems to have proven true: *forty* years later, most seminarians seem not to know the book at all.

And that is surely unfortunate! For not only is *Honest to God* a more responsible statement of the problematic confronting post-Christendom Christianity than are many of the works that have followed in its wake; it made a truly valiant effort, however sketchy, to lay hold of some of the most exciting theology of the first half of the twentieth century and cause it to speak to the church—an effort undertaken, unfortunately, by very few among both the teaching and writing theologians themselves and the parish and higher clergy. I regard it as the great ecclesiastical disaster of the twentieth century that the unprecedented renewal of profound Christian theology that occurred from about 1910 until 1960 *never reached the people in the pews*— especially not in North America.[45] Robinson's book, though by no means itself profound, on account of its immense popularity was the most significant attempt to overcome this misfortune.[46]

[44] *Christian Century* (June 24, 1964): 830.

[45] See my *Remembered Voices: Claiming the Legacy of Neo-Orthodoxy* (Louisville, Ky.: Westminster John Knox Press, 1999).

[46] In this sense, John Bennett's words may be thought prophetic: Robinson's book "can be criticized academically, but as an event it is most welcome. It has stimulated more discussion of theology in the English-speaking world than any book in years. Many readers have been introduced to thinkers from whom they may learn much more than *Honest to God* tells them." Bennett, "A Most Welcome Event," 201.

If, beyond the changes it wrought in a grateful minority within the churches, it did not succeed in altering significantly the course of twentieth-century ecclesiology, its failure to do so cannot be laid at the doorstep of its author.

As I maintained at the outset, the churches were just not ready for this book. Why? Because it "wanted to make them serious."[47] In 1963, the *still*-mainline churches were as yet able to play the role of "culture religion" (Peter Berger). The majority of those who frequented them, often or sometimes or once in a while, were not in the mood to become earnest and articulate about matters of faith. Business-as-usual kept most middle-class congregations and their clergy from any concerted effort actually to *understand* what they purported to believe, let alone subject themselves to "Teutonic" angst over the discrepancy between their religious conventions and their daily lives.

Today, however, the situation is rather different in many if not most of our *once*-mainline churches. The secular world that Robinson wrote of has blatantly invaded our consciences and our sanctuaries; religious pluralism, forty years ago present but hardly visible, is with us at every turn; our young find less and less to keep them in church. And so forth! To remain *un*serious—merely conventionally connected—in and around these old, dwindling denominations today is to invite the question: Why bother?

For that reason, if for no other, John Robinson's *Honest to God* could meet a need in today's congregations that was still waiting to be felt, or acknowledged, in 1963. One can only hope that it will do so, and thus achieve a purpose far worthier than that of a religious "best-seller" and instigator of a brief religious squall. Only such an eventuality could vindicate the true motives of its honest author.

[47] The allusion is to Kierkegaard: "Christianity is certainly not melancholy, it is, on the contrary, glad tidings—for the melancholy; to the frivolous it is certainly not glad tidings, for it wishes first of all to make them serious." See *The Living Thoughts of Kierkegaard*, Presented by W. H. Auden (Bloomington: Indiana University Press, 1966), 30.

HONEST TO GOD IN GREAT BRITAIN

ROWAN WILLIAMS

Archbishop of Canterbury

It was a most unlikely best-seller. It assumed that its readers would know at least something about the intellectual history of modern Europe (names like those of Kant and Feuerbach are introduced summarily, as if we would at least have heard of them before); it uses, again and again, a tone of relentless abstraction and a string of semitechnical words (supranatural-ism, theonomy, secularity . . .); and, above all, its central the-sis is elusive almost to the disappearing point. To call it a "work which almost anyone could read," as does Adrian Hast-ings in his *History of English Christianity 1920–1990*, is a bit optimistic.[1] And, as unfriendly critics pointed out, Robinson's characteristic style is to present a startling caricature of tradi-tional doctrine, apologize for overstating his case, and offer a rather dense translation into his preferred idiom, which leaves the reader unclear as to quite what status is now being ascribed either to the language with which we began or to the new version offered by the author. The pervasive problem is whether Robinson's translations effectively render the doctri-nal scheme no more than a complex metaphor for different kinds of experienced *intensity*.

So it is instructive to look, in this light, at one particular review of the book, and at Robinson's reaction to it. The young

[1] Adrian Hastings, *A History of English Christianity 1920–1990*, 3d ed. (Philadelphia: Trinity Press International, 1991), 537.

Alasdair MacIntyre was at that point in his intellectual odyssey very consciously post-Christian and post-Marxist; he had written in the early '50s a beautifully concise and clear book on Christianity and Marxism, at a time when, he says, he "aspired to be both a Christian and a Marxist," but had moved away, into a constructive and very interesting skepticism about "the relation of belief to organization."[2] Fifteen years on from the book's first publication, he notes the way in which the Christian and the Marxist frameworks obstinately survive what some think to be decisive refutation, and the relative blindness both systems share as to the degree and nature of their own conditionedness, their clumsiness in telling the difference between their fundamental insights and those aspects of their discourses that are "defensive or aggressive responses to their social situation."[3]

These, then, were the issues preoccupying MacIntyre in the early '60s; and from this perspective he begins his review, memorably, with the words: "What is striking about Dr. Robinson's book is first and foremost that he is an atheist."[4] He is able, without too much difficulty, to show that Robinson repeatedly uses language whose plain meaning is that theology seeks to describe what human beings are and no more; but he goes on to ask the deeper question of whether modern Protestant theology is "essentially atheistic."[5] His answer is twofold: The apparently more traditional idiom of Karl Barth at the very least runs the risk of leaving huge vulnerabilities exposed because it insists that we cannot argue but only submit to the divine Word. If theology is therefore bound to fail, if the divine Word is

[2] In preface to Alasdair MacIntyre, *Christianity and Marxism*, rev. ed. (New York: Schocken Books, 1968), 7.

[3] Ibid., 8.

[4] David L. Edwards, ed., *The Honest to God Debate* (London: SCM Press; Philadelphia: Westminster Press, 1963), 215.

[5] Ibid., 217.

wholly unsayable in human language, what really remains? And this leads to the second wing of the argument: What replaces theology is a rhetoric of moral seriousness, as in Tillich, for whom the real subject of theological assertions is the human psyche.

But the most searching of MacIntyre's observations relates to Bonhoeffer. When all else fails, the integrity of the Christian can be salvaged by suffering in resistance to the demonic religiosity of modern tyranny. Against the Third Reich, it makes sense to be a Christian; what makes faith possible in that context is the possibility "to relive Christ's passion" in powerless vulnerability before others and in service to others.[6] This at least defines what it is to be Christian in a way that the theological pessimism of Barth and the concealed psychologism of Tillich fail to do. But how does this perfectly genuine intensity, of tragedy and witness, relate to the actual world of disenchanted postwar Europe—to Bonhoeffer's church with its chaplaincies to the German armed forces, or Robinson's church, calculating its profits on the Stock Exchange? "Bonhoeffer's Christianity," writes MacIntyre, "is, then, intelligible only in one sort of context. Outside that context it lacks precisely any specific differentia from the way of life of sensitive generous liberals."[7] Worse, "It clothes ordinary liberal forms of life with the romantic unreality of a catacombic vocabulary."[8]

Thus the cultural situation of which *Honest to God* is a symptom is that, for the prosaic routinized life of modern Western humanity, there is no obviously plausible language for needs or goals that have to do with more than practical problem solving. But in the problem-solving world, there is an uncomfortable feeling that something has been left out; and this means that religious

[6] Ibid., 221.   [7] Ibid., 222.
[8] Ibid., 222.

language is still invoked to dignify a sense of contingency, of the overruling of fate, of fear and fascination in the presence of what isn't understood, the feeling that surely the story of my life has more substance and mystery and meaning than routine language can capture. Once we know that this is what religious language is there for, we can do something with it as adults (MacIntyre published a justly famous article in 1964 under the title "Is Understanding Religion Compatible with Believing?"). But if we indefinitely defer that recognition, we condemn ourselves to a cultural schism in which religious speech is the property of a self-absorbed minority, borrowed rather uncomfortably for social and psychological purposes somewhat at odds with what that speech is supposed to be talking about. *Honest to God,* MacIntyre is saying, is part of this deferral of truth, and it is, he hints, dangerous precisely because it offers a kind of illicit drama to the user of religious language. The liberal Christian, vaguely aware that what is being said cannot have real referential content, is encouraged to nurture a self-image as someone living at more "depth" than others, even living in some obscure way at more risk than others.

I have set out MacIntyre's critique at some length because, almost alone among the first generation of reviews and discussions, it helps the reader now to see some of the cultural appeal of Robinson's book in its context. MacIntyre's verdict overall is unsustainably harsh in regard to Robinson's theological position (and I shall return to this); but he quite rightly pinpoints the consonance between *Honest to God* and a generation of readers for whom the rhetoric of intensity was profoundly attractive. Robinson's reply to MacIntyre does not do a great deal to clarify the difficulties, and rather suggests that he has not taken the point about rhetoric. We read that the real issue between believer and unbeliever is "whether one can speak of ultimate reality at all and . . . what character this reality has"; and this is given a bit more specificity when Robinson rephrases it in terms of whether "Jesus's relationship to the reality he could only address as 'Abba! Father!' is veridical or not" and whether "the constitution of the universe [is] such that it justifies" trust like that of Jesus.[9] But this leads to MacIntyre's anxiety about whether this is just claiming for the religious believer a more profound experience of the same environmental data. The danger is that faith becomes a claim to seriousness, the effect of this being to foreclose any debate about discerning between kinds of seriousness, their sustainability or utility or communicability. Faith must surely be more than just an assertion that the believer is more morally interesting than the unbeliever.

The problem in *Honest to God* has a lot to do with a somewhat uncritical use of Tillich, for whom the quality of unconditional self-commitment is repeatedly made the focus of reflection. Discussing Tillich, Robinson says that what makes a statement theological is the degree to which it deals with issues around the ultimate significance of our lives.[10] Robinson clearly agrees to a large extent, but it is again not too clear whether any intensity at all will do or whether it needs to be an intensity directed toward "the personal." And in the pages that follow this bold redefinition of theology, Robinson is anxious to put some distance between himself and the Feuerbachian notion that language about God is always and only disguised language about humanity; love, intense personal attention, discloses what is fundamental in the universe but doesn't simply *constitute* it.[11] I think he wants to say that love is fundamental because of the character of "being itself"—and he is prepared, as in the chapter on Jesus that follows, to speak of some sort of revelation of

⁹ Ibid., 230.

¹⁰ John A. T. Robinson, *Honest to God* (London: SCM Press; Philadelphia: Westminster Press, 1963), 49.

¹¹ Ibid., 53.

this, some kind of transparency to what is most ontologically basic, in the life of Christ. Yet there is obvious difficulty in explaining why a sense of the supreme significance of inter-personal attention and respect requires any statement about the universe as such, let alone being as such, whatever.

Both Tillich and Robinson are, of course, battling against what they see as a false and trivializing account of what theology is: it cannot be that theology is simply a set of speculations about a putative member of the class of things that there happen to be.[12] A good many reviewers, with varying degrees of exasperation, pointed out that classical theology repeatedly denied that God was a member of any class whatsoever; the God of the *Summa*, the *Institutes,* or indeed, as David Jenkins noted, the Byzantine Liturgy is anything but a putative individual alongside others.[13] But what Tillich and Robinson are pointing us to is a situation in which theological method has become stale, if not corrupted. If God is indeed what the patristic and scholastic tradition insists God is, that is, the pure act of being, the life beyond categoriza-tion or definition that sustains all particular forms of determinate existence in the coherence of a universe, then theology certainly shouldn't be reduced to a kind of science fiction, dealing with the imagined life of some individual outside the "normal" bound-aries of experience. However, that is how theology regularly degenerates; and when Nietzsche spoke of theological discourse as simply a habit of talking about unreal causes and unreal out-comes, he identified once and for all the risk for theology of becoming just such a fictional discourse, breeding contempt for the real—a "conspiracy against life."

What could save theology from such a charge? Only a renewed sense that theological language is a difficult, always

---

[12] See, for example, ibid., 29–30.
[13] Edwards, *The Honest to God Debate*, 195.

incomplete, corruptible, but unavoidable enterprise, pressed into existence by the particular character of what God is perceived as doing, by the sense of a givenness or gratuity bearing on the human situation in such a way that a difference is made that demands new words and concepts. Now this is not, by a very long way, the idiom of *Honest to God*: one of the most startling absences in the book as a whole is surely its reluctance to speak of God as active in any way analogous to the way the word is normally used. It is particularly notable that the chapter on "Worldly Holiness" discusses prayer in terms quite divorced from any consideration that God might act on the praying person; prayer is, once again, a level of intensity within the ordinary business of interpersonal communication ("I am really praying for people, agonizing with God for them, precisely *as* I meet them and really give my soul to them.")[14]

But what is significant is the background poverty of thinking about both theology and prayer that provokes Robinson's impatience with traditional form and language in either. It is as if there is no currency for any idea that theology might exist because of the surprising new availability of kinds of prayer in the Christian community; or that there is a narrative of divine action that gives shape to our own action and our praying. To be very specific, the centrality of the doctrine of God as Trinity is nowhere to be found; with the result that the Christology is in fact remarkably abstract. Jesus gives insight into God at work, decisive insight; but it is not clear in what sense he enables a new form of relation to the source of divinity. Despite the tantalizing phrase in Robinson's reply to MacIntyre about whether Jesus' relation to God as Father is "veridical," nothing is explored in this connection that would quite bring out why the eternal intimacy and reciprocity between the source of Godhead

[14] Robinson, *Honest to God*, 99.

and the outflowing of the Godhead, the Father and the Son, should be a cardinally important way of "holding" what it is that happens in prayer. But my point is that Robinson writes as though such a question were wholly unfamiliar. He doesn't polemicize against this sort of language; indeed, he barely mentions Trinitarian doctrine. His targets in "traditional" theology are both cruder and vaguer. And unfortunately what this implies is that the bulk of the theology Robinson is regularly thinking of is crude and vague, a discourse that appears to be descriptive of a supraworldly agent.

Looking back, it is plain that the postwar period was not nearly such a wilderness from the point of view of robust doctrinal exposition and exploration as this might suggest. Gregory Dix, Austin Farrer, and Eric Mascall had all produced work that represented an amazingly creative reworking of classical themes. Dix's *Shape of the Liturgy* offers, in the course of an encyclopedic essay on liturgical development, what is actually a very comprehensive theology of Trinity and incarnation, and the restoration of human personhood and human community in the Eucharist. We might recall his description of the *homo eucharisticus* who is raised up by grace to set against the *homo economicus*, or the consumer in the Mass who is presupposed by the working practices and the advertising culture of modernity.

Farrer had at almost the same time been completing a monumental discussion of theological metaphysics and went on in the postwar period to elaborate (and endlessly revise) his thesis about will as the fundamental analogy for understanding what might be involved in ascribing personal being to God.[15] His brief essays on doctrinal themes are invariably both original and traditional.

In 1946, Mascall, already enjoying a deserved reputation as

[15] Austin Marsden Farrer, *Finite and Infinite: A Philosophical Essay* (London: Dacre Press, 1949; 2d ed., 1959).

an expositor of French Thomism, produced a book of doctrinal synthesis, *Christ, the Christian and the Church,* which spells out a coherent and immensely lively dogmatics focused on a rigorous Trinitarian and Christological schema and giving exemplary weight to the fact that the New Testament assumes the point of Christ's work to be incorporation into his relation with the Father.[16]

But if the immediate postwar period witnessed such an explosion of first-class Anglican doctrinal reflection, still fresh and suggestive more than fifty years later, it rather looks as though the '50s had forgotten why any of this mattered. It is in any case significant that the actual enterprise of dogmatics, to use the normal and somewhat forbidding term, was not part of the English university curriculum in theology for the most part. Dix was not a conventional academic theologian; Farrer was professionally a philosopher; Mascall's teaching in the '50s was likewise primarily philosophical. It could reasonably be said that, despite the extraordinary character of the work that appeared in the mid-'40s, there was practically no community of intellectual discourse that allowed the insights of these writers to be discussed and refined. British university theology outside Scotland remained dominated by biblical studies, patristics, and "philosophical theology"; no shortage there of materials for doctrinal work, but such work would have had to be done— from the academic point of view—informally. Add to this the cultural situation of the Church of England in the '50s, with its renewed institutional confidence, its mildly anti-intellectual leadership, and its half-conscious complicity in the "end of ideology" mood in the wider intellectual climate, and it is not surprising that the theological attempt to define a place to stand within a narrative of divine action was not high on the corporate Anglican agenda.

[16] E. L. Mascall, *Christ, the Christian and the Church: A Study of the Incarnation and Its Consequences* (New York: Longmans, Green, 1946).

In a sense this confirms MacIntyre's point by another route. Anglican, especially Anglo-Catholic, theology had to a degree flourished in an environment of political and cultural crisis—the '30s and early '40s. It had mattered intensely as a political thing what models of human nature were to prevail; and the war had, in the eyes of many, once again exposed the emptiness of intellectual modernity and social optimism. Some serious Anglican thinkers at least flirted with Barth, the foremost example probably being Donald MacKinnon. In crisis, the need is for resources to resist. Robinson could have found something of a crisis theology on his doorstep as a young theologian, however different its idiom is from Bonhoeffer. But the general anti-ideological tone of the '50s was hardly calculated to preserve any sense of why and how these issues had been important; and Robinson was, paradoxically, very much a child of the '50s in his intellectual style at this point.

Hence the curious tone of nervous jocularity in discussing the theological tradition. No one remembers why doctrines once had a force other than tamely descriptive; the pressure to clarify theological anthropology in unabashed dependence on grace is largely absent. Thus the nuance and qualification, the considerable subtlety of a book like Mascall's on Christology and the church simply does not register. The motivation for dogmatic excitement, both spiritual and cultural, has become obscure. You could sum up the problem by saying that the good has become obvious in a postideological situation. In such a situation, the question of what distinguishes a believer from an unbeliever is quite hard to answer except in terms of intensity: the believer has no different conception of the good, but does have a more profoundly engaged relation to it, seeing it "at depth," to use Robinson's favorite metaphor.

Let me try to put this a little differently. The Church of England in the '50s was mostly unaware of any elements of brooding crisis in its environment—and it can hardly be blamed, given the measurable signs of stability and success. But because this lessened any pressure to define clearly the rationale of its distinctive existence as church, there was actually not very much of what could strictly be called theology. By the beginning of the '60s, however, the complacent sense of not having to justify oneself was under heavy challenge as the society overall moved toward a more comprehensive consumerization. When the marketplace increasingly dominates, providers of services need to know what they're about. Less starkly, it is clear enough from Robinson and others that the lack of self-critical awareness in the institutional church in England was becoming an embarrassment, even a scandal. Hence the passionate desire to reclothe Christian commitment with the dignity of risk, depth, or whatever. But the difficulty that *Honest to God* makes plain is that, without some account of how exactly the narrative of God's action discerned by faith questions and reshapes the self's imagining of itself, the distinctive mark of faith will always be in danger of becoming no more than its own asserted human depth, sincerity, or seriousness.

This is not necessarily to say that only a conscious recovery of the classical confessional tradition can avoid such a trap, with its high risk of turning theology into a self-dramatizing exercise. There are radical alternatives (and Robinson himself famously said in the preface to *Honest to God* that he expected it to be seen in retrospect as not radical enough). In the same year that Robinson's book was published, Werner and Lotte Pelz, refugees from central Europe and already authors of a highly original and searching essay on the prophets, "True Deceivers," published *God Is No More*—the title being, characteristically, an allusion to William Blake ("Thou art a Man; God is no more").[17] Compared with *Honest to God*, its impact was minimal,

[17] Werner and Lotte Pelz, *God Is No More* (London: Gollancz, 1963).

partly because it was so densely written, partly because its authors were appreciably less well known than Robinson (though Werner Pelz had worked for some of his life as an Anglican priest). It is a very hard book to classify; the authors deliberately do not set out to redefine the doctrinal tradition, to take sides on issues of biblical historicity, or to propose a program for the reform of the church. They are ironically detached about all such issues—even about the issue of whether one should or should not say that God "exists"; what remains is the *hope* expressed in the words of Jesus, the hope he called "God," but which we must learn to call whatever we can (including perhaps "God").[18] His hope is in the strictest sense incredible and impossible: it is that human beings will become capable of living without self-justification, and thus become free for forgiveness because they are focused on the neighbor, not on the self that cries out to be told that it is good. "The words of Jesus ask us to jump over our shadow or, more correctly, to forget it. . . . [O]nly in a friend—not in a shadow, however exalted the name we give it—shall we meet the unexpected, the imponderable that astonishes us and recreates us."[19] The neighbor must become friend and the friend becomes the only possible concrete manifestation of God. In such a relation, we are not promised harmony and fulfillment, because it must be an adult and a complex matter for people who are equally on the way to something always still to be achieved; it is not about "peace as the world understands it," but about engaging with the solidity of the neighbor quite apart from the neighbor's ability to fulfill my expectations for being made to feel safe or good.[20]

Jesus is "unforgivable" for three reasons: He does not give us a "law," but himself; he relativizes or diminishes all that I think

18 Ibid., 119.   19 Ibid., 37.
20 Ibid., 78–81.

of as my achievement; and he fails, he dies, as if his hope is, after all, nonsense. The paradox is that only because of Jesus can we become free to forgive Jesus, to let him live (or make him live?). If we can receive him, not a law or a doctrine, if we can forget the problem of our achievement, if we can understand that there is no final failure so long as witness is given to the hope expressed (incarnated?) once and for all in Jesus, we forgive and are forgiven and become a means of life to one another.[21]

Such a summary gives little sense of the eloquence and freshness of the Pelzes' remarkable book; but it may at least suggest some of the differences between this work and *Honest to God*. The Pelzes share Robinson's move toward identifying the service of God and the presence of God with relation to the neighbor; but the pivotal point is not the intensity of feeling toward the neighbor but the discovery of how the search to justify the self becomes irrelevant in attention to the human other. And the significance of Jesus has little to do, in the Pelzes' book, with his transparency to a universally present love at the root of the universe's existence, but rather with his "transcendence" of the questions we ask and with the fact that his words are "never grasped, understood, fulfilled."[22] Christian identity for the Pelzes seems both more and less "secular" than for Robinson: they have no particular anxieties about reshaping a metaphysical idiom for God, and the book is a long way from anything like an ecclesiastical agenda (though it has some powerfully suggestive thoughts on the meaning of the Eucharist). But the governing images are clearly marked by the sense of being addressed, interrupted, by the words of Jesus, and summoned to a reimagining of yourself. Jesus makes something possible. It is always unachieved as soon as we start to find words for it or

---

[21] Ibid., 131–38.   [22] Ibid., 14.

reflect on our performances in relation to it. But there is a pervasive awareness of some sort of gratuity presented to us.

Robinson is far more consciously working within a framework of liturgy and doctrine, even while arguing for drastic reinterpretation. Yet, as noted earlier, there is relatively little sense of an agency beyond the sum of human agencies, and thus of a gift bestowed. The chapter on "'The New Morality'" in *Honest to God* seems to suggest that there remains a right answer to ethical dilemmas, and that this is provided by "love," which "has a built-in moral compass, enabling it to 'home' intuitively upon the deepest need of the other."[23] This contrasts sharply with the Pelzes' concern with letting go of justification (even by love) and their awareness of the labor of creating friendship in the response to the neighbor and of the ineradicability of some kinds of enmity. The surface of the two arguments has something in common; deeper down, there are very different agendas at work, that of the Pelzes perhaps more typically European in its sense of the tragic and its Lutheran passions about justification.

I am not trying to say that *God Is No More* is right and *Honest to God* wrong, but only to note one example of restoring some substance to the distinction of believer from unbeliever without simply appealing to the believer's superior moral intensity. The Pelzes may sound as if that is what they are interested in, but the whole discussion of justification gives content to the intensity in a way hard to discern in Robinson and his mentor Tillich. Yet, as I have intimated, content may also be restored by some sort of reclaiming of the doctrinal tradition itself. In the '60s, there was little sign of this; and up to the later '70s it remained true that the consensus of Anglican academic theology was not too sympathetic to the idea that creedal formulations might be a fruitful way into discussing the crises of modernity. The 1976 report of the

[23] Robinson, *Honest to God*, 115.

Doctrine Commission of the Church of England, *Christian Believing,* probably represented the high-water mark of this detachment from doctrinal tradition; much of it was a long way from Robinson's concerns, and it certainly did not echo the Tillichian and Bultmannian rhetoric of authenticity. But it can be read as one of the outcomes of the processes of which *Honest to God* was such a significant part, the processes of forgetting that the language of classical doctrine originated in the sense of a gift of transformation or conversion.

Several things were stirring by 1976 that would change the landscape further. The enormous new interest in the history of Christian spirituality, the popularity of writers like Thomas Merton, and the beginnings of a new interest in the Christian East made the 1960s' models of "worldly holiness" look a little thin. In a way wholly typical of his intellectual generosity and spiritual sensitivity, Robinson himself, in his *Exploration into God,*[24] had already begun to think through some of these issues (it is intriguing that he made such use of the Romanian novelist Petru Dumitriu in this work; Dumitriu was to publish some years later a personal account of his return to a rather unconventional Christian faith, showing a complex relationship to the Eastern Orthodox heritage of his country).

But there was also a rapidly growing interest in the theology of Continental Europe: English translations of Bultmann and Bonhoeffer no longer satisfied younger theologians looking for a fuller understanding of how the history of the mid-century had impacted European theology. The work of Jürgen Moltmann was being translated by 1970 and had immense impact. By the late '70s, more theologians were turning back to Barth for inspiration. In the whole of this process, the issues of Christian

---

[24] John A. T. Robinson, *Exploration into God* (Stanford, Calif.: Stanford University Press, 1967).

anthropology and the doctrine of God as Trinity were coming more and more into the center of intellectual concern. By the early '80s, *Honest to God* seemed a museum piece; the philosophical and doctrinal idioms regarded by Robinson and many of his generation as speculative indulgences had become keystones in all kinds of ambitious new constructions.

It would make a tidy and satisfying tale if we could simply say that *Honest to God* was a transient phenomenon at a time of rapid change and intellectual deracination in the church. It certainly breathes a cultural optimism very much of its day and a psychological naïveté in regard to its moral concerns. The wonderful question put into the mouth of a '60s cartoon character (Charlie Brown in *Peanuts*), "How can I be wrong if I'm so sincere?" sums up an entire cultural moment in a way that can't easily be improved on. But the work's significance cannot be dismissed so swiftly and patronizingly. The very unclarity about the doctrine of God that some reviewers (not least Thomists like Mascall and Herbert McCabe) deplored is actually deeply instructive. Robinson was emphatically right to observe that, whatever theologians might say, a huge amount of both popular and sermonic talk about God did indeed treat God as a member of the class of things that there are in the universe; and some of the enthusiastic retrieval by theologians in the '80s and '90s of versions of the dogmatic tradition is far less sensitive than Robinson to this problem (look, for example, at some of the really remarkable assertions about gendered language for God sometimes advanced by would-be traditionalists).

One of the major challenges to any restatement or defense of the classical creedal theology is the task of tracing the divine action in revelatory history without reinstating a fundamentally mythological idiom for speaking of that divine action. The temptation to argue for a "biblical" theology in which there are no problems in ascribing to God an action that is episodic and temporal, in treating God as, effectively, an agent among other agents in time, has been strong for many, sometimes reinforced by a superficial reading of Barth. *Honest to God* was not mistaken in diagnosing a problem and pointing out the dangers of fairy-tale language. Where I think it is inadequate in its analysis is in supposing that the difficulty comes from new cultural factors. We are told that it has become impossible to believe this or that because of changes in philosophy or science. A more nuanced understanding would note that Christian theology from at least the third century has been aware of the problem and seen it as intrinsic to all attempts to speak of God as active. The Dominican philosopher Gareth Moore, in his luminous essay on *Believing in God,* reiterates the Thomist principle that creation is not any kind of process: that something comes into being and that God created it amount to the same; the existence of the being is the act of God.[25] This is not a response to new difficulties posed by modernity, but a restatement of venerable principles.

But, venerable as they may be, they are no more currently recognized than in 1963 in the realm of professional and semiprofessional theology. Robinson's protests are intelligible, even if, to quote Herbert McCabe, "the book suffers a good deal from the author's lack of acquaintance with the history of theology."[26] Reading the book now can still awaken a fresh awareness of the problem: the fact that it is difficult to talk about God and that an unexamined discourse purporting to be about the doings of a super-worldly individual is a dangerous substitute for real theology.

A good deal of what I have been trying to suggest in these pages relates to MacIntyre's challenge to Robinson: Is the language of *Honest to God* essentially secular substance in "catacombic"

[25] Gareth Moore, *Believing in God: A Philosophical Essay* (Edinburgh: T. & T. Clark, 1988), 279.
[26] Herbert McCabe, in *The Honest to God Debate,* 166.

rhetoric? Whatever Robinson's purposes, there is some uncomfortable plausibility to the charge, especially in what I believe to be the weakest chapters of the book (on prayer and on ethics). But because he does not have a language capable of saying something about the objectivity of God without suggesting anthropomorphism, because he is not too familiar with the kind of self-critical realism of some of his Thomist reviewers, he has no clear way of distinguishing the active existence of God from what is simply "at the heart" of the universe. That God is God without respect to the universe's existence is not, for Robinson, easy to state. But I am in little doubt that this is what he would have regarded as a necessary condition of all that he does find to say of God; and his later work bears this out. I don't think that he is in this sense a forerunner of the antirealists of more recent times—Don Cupitt and his followers. My concern is rather that the lack of a robust spiritual contextualizing of doctrinal language, a lack entirely explicable in the atmosphere of the theological discussions of the late '50s and early '60s, leaves the rhetoric in possession of the field at the expense of content. Donald MacKinnon wrote in 1975 a particularly searching article on Tillich and some of his contemporaries in which he charged Tillich with yielding to the temptation "of seeing himself in his own eyes as one taking upon himself the most demanding and most frightening tasks, emancipated both by the aims, and indeed by the content, of his enterprise from the discipline of a self-questioning that reaches the very substance of what he is in himself. He is always a Romantic."[27] This would be an excessively hard judgment on Robinson, whose temperamental unlikeness to Tillich undoubtedly saved him from what MacKinnon sees as a sort of posturing on the edge of the abyss; Robinson remains committed to "purifying the dialect" of a church that is not composed

[27] Donald M. MacKinnon, "Tillich, Frege, Kittel: Some Reflections on a Dark Theme," *Explorations in Theology* 5 (London: SCM Press, 1979), 135.

of a Romantic elite. Yet, when the experiential and spiritual content of doctrine has been distorted or obliterated, where is one to locate the transformation offered by faith except in the vividness of the quality of engagement with the world's tasks? And that will always have the effect of making the believer a kind of moral hero, which sits uncomfortably with any commitment to justification by faith (which is why I signal Werner and Lotte Pelz's book as a pendant to Robinson's).

Few readers may have grasped the technicalities of the book, and judging from the responses collated and discussed by Robert Towler in his study of reactions to *Honest to God*, not all that many read it as commending or endorsing Tillichian heroism.[28] The general tone of the positive reactions is one of relief at being given permission to express dismay or disillusion at the uncritical language of what I have called the semiprofessional theological world. But if we are seeking an explanation for the fantastic success of the book in terms of sales, I suspect part of the answer lies in its rhetoric of depth, sincerity, and intensity. However poorly it was understood, the notion of the moral dignity of religious belief communicated itself somehow to the reading public. But it was a belief very loosely anchored indeed to either narrative or community—the two most influential contextual issues in about 80 percent of dogmatic theology written in English since 1980. Dignity was perceived as attached to personal fervor and integrity. But these were not conceived or assessed with reference to a governing narrative (and it is perhaps in ethics that the greatest damage has been done). Robinson touched a cultural nerve, in a way unparalleled since 1963.

There is another curious and rather paradoxical aspect of the book. It was the last religious book in the United Kingdom to

[28] See Robert Towler, *The Need for Certainty: A Sociological Study of Conventional Religion*. International Library of Sociology (London: Routledge & Kegan Paul, 1984).

have anything that could remotely be called a mass readership. In that sense, just as Luther is the last of the Rhineland mystics, so Robinson is the last of the mass religious authors. *Honest to God* is in that sense part of the very phenomenon whose decline or decadence prompted its writing. Its popularity reflects a cultural situation in which the affairs of the Church of England in particular could still attract media attention that was not simply anecdotal or prurient—and in which a measure of literacy about the Bible and about religious issues in general might be expected in the educated reading public. But what motivates Robinson is just the sense that this cultural interest is stretched as thinly as it will go, as more and more people find the church's idiom inaccessible or absurd. If the culture is in any sense to be saved for the church, the church must learn to speak in other ways. The effect is, arguably, to let the culture of the early '60s set the agenda all too firmly. Yet the underlying concern is, again, intelligible, especially given the sense of bereavement felt by a church whose involvement in the public life of the national culture had been recently pretty strong and whose official involvement remained (and remains) very visible.

Honest to God could only have been written by an Anglican at such a moment in history—which tells us much about Anglicanism in its home territory and much about that moment. Perhaps it could only have been written by someone who, like Robinson, had been at the center of academic and ecclesiastical establishment, yet was blessed with a mind never content with establishment solutions. It is not in the usual sense a "great book"; its flaws are too evident, and it does not make a coherent and original contribution to its subject matter. Yet it is the book of a great man, a lovable and faithful servant of Christ as many (including myself) will willingly testify. And there is a kind of stature in its "iconic" (to use an unhappy jargon term) status as crystallizing some of the intellectual self-doubt of '60s'

Christianity. I have tried to identify the ways in which it continues to pose utterly necessary questions—by what it says and by what it fails to say—and I am convinced that it will go on bearing fresh readings for a very long time yet. It leaves us above all with the question, MacIntyre's question, of how a language of faith rooted in experiences and expressions of "extremity" can be rendered in a bourgeois environment without self-serving drama. And if it reminds us of the dangers (for the churches as for everyone else) of an "end of ideology" intellectual culture, an abdication from the critique of our cultural constructions of the self in public and private relations, it will be salutary reading indeed.